Early Childhood Education

Sheryl O'Sullivan Smyser, Ed. D.

Teacher Created Materials, Inc.

Table of Contents

Introduction

The field of early childhood education is rapidly growing and changing. And the theory and methods used in preschools and kindergartens are having an increasing influence on the way in which the primary grades are conducted. Indeed, many early childhood practices are beginning to be espoused in the intermediate grades and beyond.

Early childhood educators have long been advocates of child-centered classrooms which encourage choice and conversation. They have structured concrete, hands-on activities which are process oriented. They have paid particular attention to structuring a stimulating environment and functioning as a guide rather than the director in that environment. And they have emphasized the use of authentic assessment in an atmosphere of acceptance. These are the very principles which are finding increasing favor in elementary and secondary schools today.

This book is designed to be a brief overview of the field of early childhood education. This includes the historical and philosophical foundations of education for young children, the work of several developmental theorists and how these relate to developmentally appropriate practice, and ways to design an appropriate and stimulating environment. The early childhood curriculum is discussed with particular attention being paid to early literacy instruction. Finally, the topics of assessment for young children and how to forge positive home-school relationships are included. This book will benefit any teacher, administrator, or parent who wishes to know more about how young children learn and how adults can encourage this learning.

Overview of Early Childhood Education

What Is Early Childhood?

There is nothing so compelling as the face of a young child. We look into those trusting, inquisitive eyes and want to do anything possible to help them grow and mature into wisdom. Throughout history this has been the goal of early childhood education, but the methods used to reach this goal have sometimes been startlingly different. In order to begin the study of what early childhood education can be in your school, we first need to look at what early childhood education has meant in the past and how we have arrived at the various interpretations of early childhood now present in our society.

Early childhood education has traditionally been divided into three distinct age groups with different programs available to each group. The preschool group usually refers to ages three and four. These children might attend nursery schools, preschools, or prekindergartens. While there are some federally funded programs available, and while there are rare instances of pre-kindergartens which are a part of the public school system, most programs for three- and four-year olds are privately funded. This means that the philosophies, methods, and quality of these programs will vary widely

> Early childhood education has traditionally been divided into three distinct age groups with different programs available to each group.

1

The second grouping within early childhood education contains the five- and six-year-old students who attend kindergarten. Kindergartens are available in the public schools, although attendance is not always compulsory. Kindergartens are also often connected to nursery schools or preschools so that children who attend these programs transition to public schools in the first grade.

The final group which is referred to as early childhood includes the six-to-eight-year-old students who are generally in grades one through three. Public education is available to all of these students. The students in the three-to-eight-year-old range are all included in the early childhood label because they share many developmental characteristics and needs. However, the classrooms of students in grades one through three increasingly resemble the classrooms in the intermediate grades more than they resemble preschool and kindergarten classrooms.

> **The students in the three-to-eight-year-old range are all included in the early childhood label because they share many developmental characteristics and needs.**

These age and program delineations are the common ones in this country today, and they are based upon a rich history of theorists who have made the education of young children a matter of priority. After reading the work of these theorists, we can identify areas of our present programs which are the results of their ideas. Let's now look at several of the most important people throughout the history of early childhood education and notice how their thoughts have influenced our present practices.

Historical Foundations of Early Childhood Education

As long ago as ancient Greece we find in the writings of Plato and Aristotle advocacy for the education of young children; yet, the early childhood education movement did not begin in earnest until about the mid-1600s (Ulich, 1950). At this time Johann Comenius wrote the first picture book for children. He also wrote *School of Infancy* and the *Great Didactic* which set out his thoughts on the education of the young. Comenius recommended the "school of the mother's lap" as the best way for preschoolers to learn. The family was considered the primary educator of its young children. Comenius also emphasized the importance of natural experiences and the use of pictures in teaching children under the age of six (Woodill, 1986).

About this same time in England, John Locke was also emphasizing natural methods of education. Locke published *Some Thoughts Concerning Education* in 1690, a book in which he put forth his philosophical view that children are a blank slate on which adults must write appropriate learnings. This view of the child as being neutral was actually a wide departure from and improvement on the commonly held view at the time of the child as depraved and in need of harsh discipline. Locke's philosophy began to move schools away from punitive methods (Ulich, 1950).

Jean Rousseau was the next great philosopher to address the education of young children. Rousseau believed that education started at birth. His book *Emile* was very influential as the basis for modern education. He built upon Locke's ideas about the importance of natural experiences, and he advocated experiences over direct instruction. Rousseau felt that all good came from God and that civilization merely confused and weakened humans. He advised that early education be in tune with nature, involve free play, and be in harmony with the child's physical and mental development. His ideas had enormous influence on Pestalozzi and other educational pioneers (Ulich, 1950).

By the early 1800s Heinrich Pestalozzi had begun to create preschools in Switzerland. Pestalozzi believed education must take into consideration the environment and circumstances of the family to be successful. He was most concerned about rescuing children from poverty and improving their environment. He advocated teaching children by having them observe the world around them. He developed many teaching aids and lessons and is sometimes considered the father of modern education (Hinitz, 1981).

The father of kindergarten is generally considered to be Friedrich Froebel.

The father of kindergarten is generally considered to be Friedrich Froebel. Froebel accepted and expanded upon the teaching of Pestalozzi in that he believed education was a lifelong endeavor which is best learned through concrete experiences. Froebel founded the first kindergarten in Germany in 1837. His method included songs, dances, and fingerplays. He based his teaching on the use of "gifts" and "occupations" and felt the teacher should individualize each child's learning through observation of that child. Froebel emphasized the importance of play.

Margaretha Schurz was a student of Froebel's in Germany, and when she immigrated to the United States she brought the concepts of Froebelian kindergarten with her. She opened the first kindergarten in this country (which was conducted in German) in Wisconsin in 1855. She introduced Elizabeth Peobody to Froebel's concepts, and Peobody began the first English speaking kindergarten of the United States in Boston in 1860. Both of these kindergartens were private schools. The first public kindergarten was begun by Susan Blow in 1873 through the St. Louis, Missouri, public schools. All of these kindergartens were based upon Froebelian principles. Unfortunately, due to large class sizes and the day care functions which became attached to early childhood education, many of Froebel's concepts are no longer apparent in kindergartens (Lawler and Bauch, 1988).

In this century, early childhood education has seen many changes. Patty Smith Hill adapted Froebelian concepts to include more free play and flexibility. She also was instrumental in the beginning of the two largest associations for the education of young children, the Association for Childhood Education International and the National Association for the Education of Young Children. Her philosophy

3

emphasized creativity and large muscle development.

Maria Montessori used her work with mentally handicapped children in Italy to begin her "Children's House" in 1906. Her ideas are based upon the premise that children learn best through sensory experiences. She believed the teacher should function as the facilitator of the child's learning. Montessori's method has very specific learning materials which are to be used in specific ways. Her ideas did not find wide acceptance in the United States until the 1950s and 1960s (Spodek, 1985).

In addition to the philosophers and theorists who have influenced our present view of early childhood education in this country, acts of Congress have also played an influential role in the field. Two acts have been especially important. In 1941 the Lanham Act appropriated funds to establish nursery schools for the children of mothers who were working in the war effort. And in 1965 the Elementary and Secondary Education Act funded Head Start (Hinitz, 1981). Head Start, as a preschool program for at-risk children, continues today and has spawned other educational initiatives, such as Follow Through and Home Start.

It is apparent from this brief overview of the history of early childhood education that our current practices are based upon centuries of thought about the needs of young children. Let's turn our attention in the next chapter to theories of child development and the ways in which these theories influence instruction.

Concluding Remarks

Early childhood education today is generally divided into three areas. These include preschool (ages 3–4), kindergarten (ages 5–6), and primary grades (ages 6–8). Public school programs are available for kindergarten and the primary grades, but most preschool programs are privately funded. Preschools tend to be more child based and play centered while kindergartens and primary grades are increasingly academically oriented.

A rich history undergirds present early childhood education, with the ideas of philosophers and theorists from Plato to Montessori. Also included were Comenius, Locke, Rousseau, Pestalozzi, Froebel, Schurz, Peobody, Blow, and Hill. In addition, there have been several legislative acts which have influenced early childhood education.

> Montessori's method has very specific learning materials which are to be used in specific ways.

4

Development in Early Childhood

Developmental Stages

Who are these children who populate our preschools, kindergartens, and primary grades? What are they like, and what do they need? Any discussion of developmentally appropriate practice must necessarily begin with a firm grounding in child development. Without a strong, working knowledge of how children develop between the ages of three and eight, it will be impossible to choose activities which are appropriate to their developmental needs. It is always easier to think of developmental theory by applying it to a real child, so let's meet three children of different early childhood ages.

Morgan is four and goes to preschool. She has a protruding tummy, and her growth has slowed somewhat from her infant growth spurt. She is doing a good job of gaining control of her large muscles. She can run, kick a large ball, do a forward roll, and jump up and down. She does all of these things, and many more physical activities, constantly. Morgan's small motor skills are not as good as her gross motor ones. She can use scissors and write on large paper, but the results are not always up to her standards.

> **Any discussion of developmentally appropriate practice must necessarily begin with a firm grounding in child development.**

5

Morgan has excellent language skills. She has a very large vocabulary and understands most conventional grammar. Her vocabulary is very concrete, however, and she still makes endearing mistakes with irregular verbs. She also has trouble pronouncing her l's and r's. While her articulation may lag a little, her cognitive understanding of language is strong. She is able to use language to think but still depends on her concrete perceptions rather than logic to understand problems. In other words, if the tall, skinny glass looks like it has more than the short, round glass, then it must have more.

Morgan is an active, friendly participant in her play. She sometimes plays alone but often enjoys dramatic play with other children. She has a very difficult time seeing anyone else's point of view, however, which sometimes means she will argue during playtime. She is very tenderhearted, though, and wants very much to be liked by the others. Right now a great deal of the play in her group seems focused on sex-role identification.

Whitney is a six-year-old kindergartner. While she is only one grade above Morgan, she is nearly two years older, and their developmental differences are quite noticeable. Whitney's physical skills are quite a bit better than Morgan's. She has gained improved coordination and balance and can hop, skip, jump rope, and walk on a balance beam. Her fine motor skills are also much improved. She can color, print, and cut with good dexterity and does all of these consistently with her left hand.

Whitney is undergoing a real transition in the way she is able to think. She is moving away from a dependence on her perceptions and can sometimes follow logic even if it "looks wrong." Her memory is increasing, and she can use her maturing language skills to retell stories or give information to others. Her classification skills are a big help when the blocks need to be put away according to size and shape.

Socially, Whitney is increasingly able to see other people's points of view. She enjoys games with rules now, and the increased social network of school gives her lots of opportunities for playing cooperatively with others. She enjoys doing activities at which she can be successful, which means she sometimes stays in one area of the classroom more than her teacher, who wants to encourage balanced growth, would like.

Collin is eight years old and in the third grade. Developmentally he is working on very different tasks than either Whitney or Morgan. Collin's growth has slowed down and will remain slower until adolescence. This allows him to gain increasing control over both his large and small muscles, making him more successful at physical activities. His eyesight is keener, which lets him read smaller print, and his increased small muscle coordination allows him to write legibly in a relatively small space. All of these physical developments have combined with Collin's increased mental abilities to influence the types of school tasks Collin can be expected to do. His ability to use symbols to think means he depends less on his perceptions and can read, write, and understand number concepts. He is eager to do this type of traditional schoolwork because he remains curious and wants to be productive. He is most successful in his school work, though, when the activity is concrete and uses his prior knowledge.

Socially, Collin is very interested in the concept of fairness. His idea of fairness, however, means everyone should be treated identically, and the punishment for infractions should be swift and severe. He and the other boys in his grade play endless games of soccer at recess, which often erupt into arguments over the rules. Collin may argue with his friends, but his peers are very important to him. He wants to fit in and knows exactly how his skills compare to the rest of the group.

A great deal of theoretical work has been done to study and delineate the various stages of development for children.

Theorists in Child Development

All three of these children are displaying normal developmental tendencies for their ages. All three are in school environments which respect their developmental differences and needs rather than try to inhibit them. A great deal of theoretical work has been done to study and delineate the various stages of development for children. In this section we will look at the work of several theorists and apply those ideas to the three early childhood youngsters we have just met.

Probably the most influential theorist in the cognitive development of children is Jean Piaget. Piaget was a Swiss psychologist who studied the way children view the world and how they learn. He found that children grow and mature in their thinking through the processes of assimilation and accommodation. Assimilation refers to the act of taking in new information, while accommodation means whatever activity the child has to do to make the new information fit into existing knowledge. Sometimes the new knowledge fits easily into the child's schema, and sometimes this new information will mean the child has to change something in his old thinking that no longer fits.

In using these two processes children progress through a sequence of four stages, according to Piaget (1952). The stages are sequential, are undertaken in the same order by everyone, and are never skipped. They do represent a continuum, however, so that children in one stage may display tendencies of another stage as they move through transitional times when the stages overlap.

Piaget's stages of cognitive development are listed below. The two stages of most interest to early childhood educators are the pre-operational stage (two–seven years) and the concrete operations stage (seven–eleven years). Pre-operational children are bound by their perceptions. They are not able to apply logic to problems which do not fit their physical perceptions of the world. Morgan is displaying this when she refuses to take a short, round glass of juice because it looks like she is getting less juice than her friends with tall, skinny glasses.

Piaget's Stages of Cognitive Development

◆ Sensorimotor Stage (0–2 yrs.)

learns through senses and movement

◆ Pre-operational Stage (2–7 yrs.)

egocentric, symbolic, uses perceptions to learn

◆ Concrete Operations Stage (7–11 yrs.)

uses symbols to think, has conversation, sees other points of view

◆ Formal Operations Stage (12 yrs. and up)

abstract thinking

Children at the pre-operational stage are also egocentric. This does not mean that they are selfish, but that they do not have the capacity to see another's point of view. They do not even recognize that there might be a different point of view. Morgan shows this egocentrism during her playtime arguments, but Whitney, who is transitioning between the two stages, understands different points of view well enough to begin to play games with rules.

Finally, children in the pre-operational stage cannot keep more than one attribute or idea in mind at a time. This makes all sorts of school tasks difficult for them. For instance, classifying tasks which ask students to attend to two characteristics or phonics instruction which asks for attention to both letters and sounds will be difficult for Morgan. Whitney is already displaying the ability to conserve, or think two ideas at the same time, when she organizes the blocks by size and shape.

The average child transitions from the pre-operational to the concrete operations stage between the ages of five and seven. Children of these ages will display tendencies of both stages at different times. By the age of seven, most children will have entered the concrete operations stage and will be ready for different types of instruction.

Children in the concrete operations stage do not depend so much upon their perceptions to explain reality. They can apply logic now, especially if the problem is presented in a concrete way. Collin displays his increased ability to use logic and symbols as he learns to read, write, and do math. He can now keep more than one idea at a time in mind, and understand that actions are reversible. These skills allow him to break away from a perception-bound view of the world.

Collin is also freed, to a great extent, from the egocentrism of the pre-operational stage. He may argue vehemently about fair application of the rules, but he is able to realize that someone else might see things differently. Both Collin and Whitney are able to enlarge their peer groups and enjoy cooperative play because of this decrease in egocentrism.

Kohlberg (1976) used Piaget's work with cognitive stages of development to begin looking at another aspect of growth, moral development. Kohlberg found that everyone passes through stages in the development of moral behavior. A chart delineating these stages is shown below. Early childhood students are generally in the preconventional stage, which means their behavior is largely governed from the outside. They generally obey rules to avoid punishment or to get something that they want. They do not yet care about following rules for a higher good. The egocentrism of Piaget's pre-operational stage means that young children are not capable of looking beyond what is personally good to what might be good for another.

Kohlberg found that everyone passes through stages in the development of moral behavior.

Kohlberg's Stages of Moral Development

Level 1 Preconventional (4–10 yrs.)—external control

Type 1 obeys rules to avoid punishment.

Type 2 obeys rules to get what is wanted.

Level 2 Conventional (10–13 yrs.)—external control

Type 3 obeys rules to please others.

Type 4 obeys rules to maintain social order.

Level 3 Postconventional (13 yrs. & up)—internal control

Type 5 obeys rules based on acceptable laws and individual rights.

Type 6 obeys rules based on universal ethical principles.

While Piaget and Kohlberg considered cognitive and moral development in children, Erik Erikson (1963) studied their psychosocial growth. He, too, devised a hierarchy of stages through which all pass in their social and emotional development. These stages are shown on the following page. For early childhood educators, the most important stages are the Initiative vs. Guilt and the Industry vs. Inferiority levels.

Erikson's Stages of Psychosocial Development

Stage	Age	Necessary for Success
Trust vs. Mistrust	0–1 1/2 yrs.	Needs are met
Autonomy vs. Doubt	1–3 yrs.	Success in activities
Initiative vs. Guilt	3–5 yrs.	Success with others
Industry vs. Inferiority	6–11 yrs.	Productive activity
Identity vs. Role Confusion	12–18 yrs.	Exploration of roles
Intimacy vs. Isolation	18–35 yrs.	Belonging
Generativity vs. Stagnation	35–60 yrs.	Opportunities to share
Integrity vs. Despair	60 yrs. & up	Meaning in life

Children pass through predictable stages in their development in many areas.

Morgan is still dealing with the tasks of Initiative vs. Guilt. During this stage children need to act upon their environments and meet with success in these interactions. Morgan's free play shows her curious, imaginative experiments, and to restrict this would cause her to doubt herself. In order for her to develop a sense of purpose, she needs a stimulating environment with support from adults. If she is in a constrictive environment, she will feel guilty about her yearnings and show less initiative.

Collin and Whitney are both in the Industry vs. Inferiority stage to a certain extent. Children at this stage want to learn the skills they need. School fits beautifully into this developmental stage because the primary goals of the early grades are to teach children the tools of reading, writing, and arithmetic. Children at this stage want to be competent, and they decide upon their competence by looking at the products of their work and by comparing their work with others' work. To become competent, children at this stage need to interact with the environment in ways designed to increase their skills. And, they need to experience success. If they are consistently unsuccessful, feelings of inferiority will develop, and industry will decline.

Concluding Remarks

Children pass through predictable stages in their development in many areas. In cognitive development, the work of Piaget is vitally important, with the pre-operational and concrete operations stages being the ones in which most early childhood students function. Kohlberg's stages of moral development are connected to Piaget's work. Kohlberg's preconventional stage is the level of most children in early childhood. Finally, the work of Erikson in psychosocial development places children in preschool at the Initiative vs. Guilt stage and primary students at the Industry vs. Inferiority level. It is extremely important that early childhood teachers are familiar with these various stages of child development if they are to be able to plan developmentally appropriate activities.

Developmentally Appropriate Practice

What Is Developmentally Appropriate?

Developmentally appropriate practice, or DAP for short, is one of the most widely used and consistently misunderstood terms in early childhood education today. Taking this nomenclature apart, though, we see it is not such a mystery. It merely means that our practice, or method of teaching, is chosen to be effective with the developmental levels of the children we teach. This might merely be considered a longer way to say good teaching. Indeed, while early childhood educators seem to be the only ones discussing developmentally appropriate practice, one could argue that consideration of the developmental levels of students should be the beginning point of any effective teaching, regardless of level.

While there is nothing mysterious about the term developmentally appropriate practice, it is not always an easy concept to implement. For one thing, its effective use presupposes that teachers thoroughly understand child development in general and can apply those concepts in the classroom. We cannot successfully choose activities which are developmentally appropriate without this vital theoretical knowledge. In this book, these concepts are presented in Chapter 2,

> Developmentally appropriate practice, or DAP for short, is one of the most widely used and consistently misunderstood terms in early childhood education today.

11

and you should refer back to that chapter regularly as you read the rest of the book.

In addition to a general knowledge of child development, effective implementation of DAP demands that teachers are able to identify the specific developmental needs of the individual students they teach. Developmentally appropriate practice is not a one-size-fits-all way of teaching. Children of the same age can be at radically different developmental levels. And, the same child can have very different needs in the cognitive, social, and physical domains. Determining and meeting such varied needs can be a daunting task.

A final difficulty in implementing DAP is the need for teachers to become less reliant on published curricula and become more self-reliant in organizing their classrooms. While developmentally appropriate practice is certainly child centered, it is also teacher-directed. Teachers must make judgments about the needs of their children, must determine what activities will best meet those needs, and must organize those activities in an integrated and sensible way. This necessitates that early childhood educators have access to continuing opportunities for staff development which focus particularly on teaching young learners.

While the implementation of DAP may demand well-educated, skillful teachers with high energy, it is the general consensus of early childhood experts today that DAP is the correct philosophy when teaching young children. David Elkind in his book *Miseducation: Preschoolers at Risk* (1987) gave public voice to the idea that traditional, skill-based classrooms were not appropriate for early childhood education. The National Association for the Education of Young Children has issued numerous policy documents on appropriate education for children up to the age of eight. Other associations, such as NAESP and ASCD, have subsequently issued their own policy statements in support of developmentally appropriate practice. Rarely has one philosophy or method of teaching been embraced so completely by a profession. So, while teaching using DAP is not effortless, it is well grounded in research and worth the energy it will take to implement.

Components of DAP

Developmentally appropriate practice has several components which can be implemented into any classroom. Teachers should keep in mind as they implement these components, though, that the premise of DAP is to use the developmental levels of children to inform classroom practice. Incorporating the following components into a classroom will not produce developmentally appropriate practice if the needs of the students are not the beginning point of instructional planning.

> **Developmentally appropriate practice has several components which can be implemented into any classroom.**

Concrete

Young children learn best through concrete manipulation of materials. They do not profit from lecture-type teaching or anything needing abstract thinking. They need to have their own materials and be allowed to act on those materials to solve their own problems (Weikert, Rogers, Adcock, and McClelland, 1971). This is based upon Piagetian theory which states that early childhood students are in the pre-operational stage and must use all of their senses in an active way to learn efficiently. This means that math manipulatives, hands-on science investigations, small-motor activities, and dramatic play areas should be provided.

Active

Anyone who has tried to keep young children seated and quietly engaged for a long period of time knows the futility of this. Yet, traditional school-age programs ask children to do just that, and often in an attempt to imitate older grades, preschools and kindergartens also require extended seat time and paper and pencil tasks. Not only will this be frustrating to both teacher and student, but it is an inefficient way of learning for young children. Children learn best through active engagement with their environment. This active engagement is often called play outside of the classroom and has somehow been labeled as a waste of time. But play is anything but a waste of time. It is the optimal way in which young children learn. Sutton-Smith (1967) linked play with cognitive development. And Parten (1933) established the link between play and social development.

Active learning and the use of concrete manipulatives mutually enhance each other in the developmentally appropriate classroom. The emphasis shifts from the teacher having all of the materials and getting to do all of the activities to the children having their own materials and acting upon them. An example of this is illustrated by a cooking activity in a kindergarten. In the less active program the teacher bakes bread by having the children watch and occasionally lend assistance. In a more appropriate approach each child has a butter tub in which to mix the ingredients, and each child kneads and bakes an individual roll.

An active learning environment will naturally foster another ingredient necessary for the growth of young children, and that is social interaction. Children in early childhood programs learn best together by experimenting on their environment and talking about what happens. An active learning atmosphere will encourage conversation and cooperation which are so necessary for language development and social growth. An idea list of times when cooperative learning could be incorporated is on the following page.

Young children learn best through concrete manipulation of materials.

13

Cooperative Learning

There are many times when using cooperative learning partners or groups in kindergarten are appropriate. Some suggestions are given below.

Literature
- ❖ Tell a partner a favorite part of the story.
- ❖ Draw a picture together of their favorite part of a story on one piece of paper.
- ❖ Act out the story together.
- ❖ Put together a puzzle of the story with a partner.
- ❖ Read the story together, using one book and taking turns, and then tell each other the story.
- ❖ Use the blocks and build something from the story.
- ❖ Tell a flannel board story together, etc.

Math
- ❖ Use the math tubs with a partner and do sorting, patterns, measuring, and making sets.
- ❖ Read the calendar (number line) with a partner.

Music
- ❖ Use the instruments with a partner.
- ❖ Teach a partner a favorite song.
- ❖ Teach a partner a dance.
- ❖ Sing together.

Science
- ❖ Do an experiment together and draw a picture about the experiment together.
- ❖ Find a book about a science area both partners like and look at the book together.
- ❖ Discuss it and draw a picture about it to share with the class.

Art
- ❖ Draw, color, or paint a picture together.
- ❖ Use play dough and make something with a partner.
- ❖ Finger paint a picture with a partner.

Physical Education
- ❖ Play ball with a partner.
- ❖ Turn a jump rope with a partner and have another group jump.
- ❖ Teach a partner a favorite game.
- ❖ Share the physical education toys with a partner.
- ❖ Take turns pulling a partner in a wagon, etc.

Other Areas
- ❖ Room environment
- ❖ Focus on social competency
- ❖ Daily routines
- ❖ Structure of lessons
- ❖ Parents/cross-age tutors

There are many areas of the curriculum in which to use cooperative learning. As you gain experience, more ideas will come. Integrate the curriculum with cooperative skills.

Reprinted from TCM 516 How to Manage Your Kindergarten Classroom, *Teacher Created Materials, 1995*

Choice

Developmentally appropriate practice seems like an impossible way to teach if we focus on all of the many individual needs of a class of students and ponder how to meet those needs one at a time. One characteristic of a DAP classroom makes this much more feasible, however. This is the concept of allowing children to choose how and what they will learn. By building a stimulating, engaging, and purposeful learning environment and then allowing children to make choices within that environment, teachers can accommodate individual developmental needs fairly easily. Children are quite wise about their own learning. They know what they are curious about and are nearly impossible to deter when it comes to seeking out the knowledge they need. They seem to know instinctively how to acquire information at a level at which it will be useful to them. Providing choice in the early childhood classroom takes advantage of this natural ability.

Curriculum Integration

Young children learn about the world in an integrated way.

Young children learn about the world in an integrated way. They do not learn science concepts apart from language in an atmosphere that ignores social skills. Yet in many traditional classrooms, this is just how curriculum is arranged. Reading, spelling, science, mathematics, social studies, and music are taught at distinctly separate times of the day with no fluidity among the content. This fragmentation of the curriculum is not the natural way in which young children learn. Many early childhood educators advocate the use of themes and learning centers to overcome this fragmentation. Pulling all areas of the curriculum together around a theme or a piece of children's literature makes the day more logical for children and allows them to connect new learning with prior knowledge. Learning centers not only allow for curriculum integration but also encourage student choice and active learning. One way for planning an integrated day is found on the next page.

	Monday	Tuesday	Wednesday	Thursday	Friday
Weekly Theme: *Families* **Week of:** _____					
Date					
Sharing Time	Poem: "Grandma's Spectacles"	Finger Play: "Baby Grows"	Finger Play: "Fine Family"	Poem: "The Family"	Poem: "I Asked My Mother"
Art	Easel Painting	Friendship Chain	Special Bouquet	Family Tree	Family Card
Story Time	Book: *Just Me and My Mom*	Book: *Just Me and My Dad*	Book: *What Is a Family?*	Book: *When the Relatives Came*	Book: *When I Was Young in the Mountains*
Circle Time	Flannel Story: "The Bundle of Sticks"	Song: "Friends"	Folk Song: "Hush, Little Baby"	Finger Play: "Good Little Mother"	Song: "What a Miracle"
Food Experiences	Family Favorites	Gingerbread Family	Family Style	Family Dessert	Take Home a Treat
Theme Activities	Book: *Love You Forever*	Flannel Story: "Old Mother Hubbard"	Song: "The Hugging Song"	Book: *Your Family Tree*	Book: *Are You My Mother?*

Reprinted from TCM 146 Early Childhood Themes Through the Year, *Teacher Created Materials, 1993*

16

Myths About Developmentally Appropriate Practice

For some reason several misconceptions about developmentally appropriate practice have been generated as the trend toward using DAP has increased. These need to be clearly understood by anyone wanting to embrace the DAP philosophy, not only so they can be avoided in practice but also so that they can be refuted as they arise.

One unfortunate misconception about DAP is that those teachers who adopt it do not really teach, and, therefore, DAP is for lazy practitioners. Nothing could be further from the truth. Teachers in developmentally appropriate classrooms are teaching constantly, albeit in a more appropriate way for the ages of their students. These teachers establish goals for learning, design and direct learning activities, and measure the success of their plans just as teachers do in more traditional classrooms. However, instead of a didactic approach to teaching, DAP teachers concentrate on building an environment conducive to meeting the goals they have for individual children. These teachers act as facilitators as their children actively engage in their own learning. In terms of energy, planning, and teacher reflection, DAP generally is much more demanding than traditional transmissive teaching.

However, instead of a didactic approach to teaching, DAP teachers concentrate on building an environment conducive to meeting the goals they have for individual children.

Another misconception about DAP is that it is non-academic and therefore less rigorous than an academic early childhood program. Again, this is incorrect. Skills, facts, and specific academic knowledge are as valued in DAP classrooms as in any other classroom. The difference is in how these skills are taught. Instead of workbook-type, discrete skill activities, academic skills in a DAP class will be taught through active, concrete, integrated activities. The teacher still has specific learning goals for the students, but these goals are accomplished in a child-centered way which is more conducive to true understanding and retention of knowledge.

Finally, developmentally appropriate classrooms are often accused of being chaotic. To the uninitiated observer this would certainly seem true. Children are active, talking, and moving from place to place. There are children doing a wide variety of activities in various learning centers throughout the room. The observer expecting to see quiet children seated at desks and attending to one activity as it is presented by the teacher will certainly judge the DAP classroom as chaotic. Of course, this is not correct. The successful developmentally appropriate class has been designed by a thoughtful teacher and is being orchestrated by that teacher to meet the assessed learning needs of the students. A closer look at the classroom will reveal the underlying diligence and order while the children are active and engaged.

Moving to a Developmentally Appropriate Classroom

Understanding the theoretical principles and the characteristics of a DAP classroom are the first steps toward changing to a more appropriate environment for young children. Most of us were not taught in this manner as children, and we had limited exposure to early childhood theories in our professional training. This shift, then, may be difficult to accomplish even if we are convinced it is the right step. One of the easiest ways to move toward a more developmentally appropriate classroom is to do it gradually by slowly changing different areas in your classroom. Here are some ideas:

One of the easiest ways to move toward a more developmentally appropriate classroom is to do it gradually by slowly changing different areas in your classroom.

◆ Add a learning center or two around your classroom. Try a dress-up corner, a science table, or an author's nook. Do this even if you teach six- to eight-year olds. Do not limit it to preschool or kindergarten.

◆ Build at least part of your curriculum around a theme. Choose a holiday, an area of study, or a children's book and unify math, social studies, language arts, and fine arts around this book.

◆ Schedule a period each day in which children can choose their own activities. Provide choices which support your curriculum during this time.

◆ For one lesson per day (at least to start) ask yourself how this learning can be accomplished in a more concrete, active way. Change one lesson at a time to be more developmentally appropriate.

◆ Consciously plan activities which encourage children to work together and talk. Or just encourage a more general atmosphere of cooperation and conversation in your classroom.

◆ Choose an academic skill you wish your children to acquire and think of a way to teach this skill other than the page of the workbook which the students would ordinarily complete. A sample lesson is included on the following page as a more concrete way to teach the skill of sequencing.

Yummy Mud Buckets

Preparation Time:
One-two hours

Language Arts and Socialization Concept:
This activity introduces three-, four-, and five-year-olds to the idea of following sequential directions.

Materials:
small, disposable heat-resistant containers (Small plastic cups shaped like small pails will work.), one for each child; chocolate pudding, enough for $\frac{1}{2}$ to $\frac{3}{4}$ of a cup (125 mL to 180 mL) for each child; several pounds of gummy worms; two boxes of graham crackers; plastic spoons; two boxes of chocolate sandwich cookies

What to Do:
In this activity children help make their own edible mud buckets, wormy pudding treats only a child could love! Children will learn to follow sequential directions, make models, and learn about nature all while preparing a "wormy" pudding treat! To prepare for this activity you will need to ensure you have a bucket and a work space for each child. While you can prepare your own pudding at school from a package or make a large bowl of it at home, it is also possible to buy prepared chocolate pudding from a regular grocery story or a restaurant supply store.

To begin this activity, talk with the children about things that live in the earth. Hold a class discussion regarding all the insects and animals that live in the earth. Mention worms, grubs, ants, moles, groundhogs, squirrels, snakes, mice, etc. Next, model the mud-bucket activity for children and let them create their own pudding buckets with assistance.

Children will love to drop in the "worms." Expect lots of laughter! Following are the steps to prepare a mud bucket:

- ❖ Use a clean bucket or cup.
- ❖ Put in a $\frac{1}{2}$ cup (120 mL) of chocolate pudding.
- ❖ Drop in several gummy worms.
- ❖ Add more pudding.
- ❖ Squish several more "worms" down in the pudding soil.
- ❖ Crunch up a handful of graham crackers. Sprinkle on top.
- ❖ Crunch up a handful of chocolate cookies. Sprinkle on top.

Reprinted from TCM 484 Everyday Activities for Preschool, *Teacher Created Materials, 1995*

Concluding Remarks

There is nothing mysterious about developmentally appropriate practice. It is merely the planning of instruction based upon the developmental needs of the students. The concept is somewhat difficult to implement, however, because it depends on a very strong understanding of child development and an attention to individual needs. It includes the components of active concrete learning, choices for children, and curriculum integration. It does not ignore the teaching of skills or take away teacher responsibility for learning. However, skills are taught in context and in concrete ways. And the teacher continues to plan and orchestrate learning, but in an active way, for the children. DAP is a well-regarded method of teaching in the early childhood community and worth the effort it takes to change from a more traditional classroom model.

The Early Childhood Classroom

Classroom Environment

Now that you are knowledgeable about child development in the early years and have given some thought to what practices are appropriate during those years, it is time to turn our attention to setting up the classroom environment in which our students will learn. This environment will include not only the physical space and materials available to children but also the daily routines, discipline techniques, and general climate of the early childhood classroom.

We have just spent several pages exploring how children mature and how classroom activities must honor children's developmental levels. However, this does not mean that we simply sit and wait for maturation and hope for the best. Indeed, we have a responsibility to help children in their development. Environment plays an important part in enabling children to reach their potentials. And early environment is especially crucial.

Benjamin Bloom (1964), in his important synthesis of numerous research studies on human development, discovered several trends which relate directly to early childhood teaching. First, he found that

> Environment plays an important part in enabling children to reach their potentials.

some characteristics of development, such as physical growth, are relatively stable. We can predict a child's adult height fairly accurately, for instance, by age two, and only extreme environmental influences will affect that. Other characteristics, though, are not as stable. Intellectual growth and the development of attitudes and values are more susceptible to environmental changes.

Second, Bloom found that humans do not develop at a constant rate. There is very rapid development in the early childhood years; this growth slows during middle childhood; then, another growth spurt takes place in adolescence. This is true in all areas of development. In addition to being able to predict a child's adult height by age two, we can predict 80 percent of a child's intellectual ability by age eight and 50 percent of his attitudes and values by age five.

If the early years are a time of immense growth, this is the time when our efforts to provide a nourishing, stimulating environment will be most effective.

Finally, Bloom discovered that the effects of the environment will be most pronounced on development during times of greatest growth. Putting all of this together, it is immediately apparent how important the early childhood environment is. If the early years are a time of immense growth, this is the time when our efforts to provide a nourishing, stimulating environment will be most effective.

What kind of environment, then, will be most nourishing? Another theorist, Vygotsky (1962), provides us with a clue. Vygotsky coined the term "zone of proximal development." By this he meant the level of development just above the level where the child is presently functioning. Vygotsky found that if children were presented with a problem just barely too difficult for them and given guidance from an adult, they could briefly function at the higher level. Eventually, they functioned more frequently at the higher stage until, finally, this became their actual developmental level.

In setting up the early childhood classroom, it is important to keep Bloom's thoughts on a stimulating environment and Vygotsky's ideas about a challenging environment in mind. To orchestrate the classroom environment, teachers must first discern what children know and do not know. Assessment is important in planning and is discussed in Chapter 7. Next, teachers need to decide what children need to learn. This all-important goal setting meshes developmental needs and curriculum expectations. Finally, teachers must design activities and situations in which children learn efficiently what they need to know.

Keeping in mind these three steps of assessment, goal setting, and activity planning, let's look at a typical physical arrangement for an early childhood classroom. A diagram of one way to arrange your room can be found on page 25. It is only one example, however, and you will want to decide upon what works best in your classroom.

The following components should be considered as you design your environment.

◆ Safety—This is the first consideration, and you should regularly examine your room for hazards. Are traffic paths clear? Are dangerous items put away? Is equipment in good repair? Ask these questions, and others like them, on a daily basis.

◆ Child centered—The room should have furniture appropriately sized to the children who will use it. The displays and work areas must be at the children's level. Children should have individual areas, such as cubbies, in which to keep their personal belongings and also group space in which to meet and work collectively.

◆ Convenient—Think clearly about the many functions which take place in your room and decide how they can best be accommodated in a small space. Noisy and quiet areas should be separated. Messy activities should be grouped together on a tile floor and near a sink, if possible. Non-messy areas will be quieter if situated in carpeted space. Traffic patterns such as the route to the door and the path to the coat room should be taken into consideration. Anything you can arrange so that children can be independent will make the day easier, so putting supplies low and making cleanup simple will be important.

◆ Inviting—Children must want to learn in this room. Keeping materials out, or on shelves where they are visible, will be motivating to children. Different levels, such as a reading loft or a gathering pit, make the room more interesting. Books, displays, and comfortable areas in which to work will invite learning.

◆ Active—Children learn most quickly through actively manipulating their environment. The areas of the room should invite children to be active by providing ample materials for each child, encouraging talking and cooperative activities, and valuing play as a means for learning.

◆ Curriculum based—Finally, the environment should be designed to achieve the curricular goals of the teacher. One way to do this is through the use of learning centers. Preschools and kindergartens are often arranged into learning centers, and these centers are generally grouped around an activity, such as the dress-up center or the block corner. Primary grades which have learn-

Children learn most quickly through actively manipulating their environment.

23

ing centers often make the areas more curriculum driven, such as the writing center or the science table. The developmentally-based early childhood classroom, regardless of level, can appropriately include both. The activities in each center will be different, of course, based upon developmental levels and needs. Some centers may be in the room all year with the activities changing. This includes the library corner or a math manipulatives table. Other centers will come and go, depending on the teaching. A dinosaur center or literature unit table would fall into this category. A listing of possible centers with suitable inclusions is on page 26.

Preparing a Classroom

Sample Room Arrangement

The following is a diagram of a developmental class set up to handle 60 children each day—30 in the morning and 30 in the afternoon. Notice where the children's cubbies are placed to facilitate traffic flow. There are many variations on setting up a room and some experimentation is necessary. After the year starts, the room arrangement may be changed after it has been evaluated. It may also be changed year to year as new ways are found to manage a classroom. Items to consider as the room is arranged include:

- traffic flow in and out of the room
- traffic flow to the bathroom and the sink (if they are in the room)
- placement of work tables
- placement of the rug if it is separate
- the bulletin board used the most with the children
- possible interest centers
- playhouse

Classroom Diagram

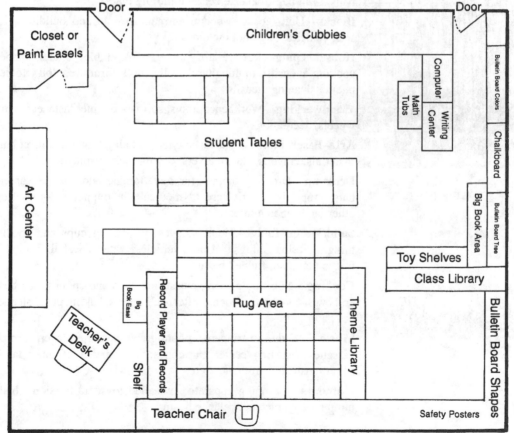

Reprinted from TCM 516 How to Manage Your Kindergarten Classroom, *Teacher Created Materials, 1995*

Integrated Learning Centers with Inclusions

Below are suggestions for learning centers in your early childhood classroom.

Reading—Comfortable spots to read, books of many levels and genres, stories on tape, children's newspapers and magazines, display areas, alphabet activities, big books

Science—Aquarium, terrarium, clock, magnets, rocks, leaves, insects, plants, egg incubator, ant farm, scale

Mathematics—Geoboard, tangrams, manipulatives to count, number activities, shape activities, seriation kits, unifix cubes, cuisenaire rods, clock

Small Motor—Puzzles, bead stringing, pegboards, parquetry blocks, lacing cards, writing materials, dressing frames, flannel board and activities, sorting activities, markers, crayons

Large Motor—Climbing apparatus, small-wheel toys, traffic signs, balls, bean bags, balance beam, tumbling mat

Blocks—Unit blocks, wooden animals, people and buildings, log sets, vehicles, large hollow blocks

Housekeeping—Refrigerator, stove, sink, table, chairs, dishes, cooking utensils, multicultural dolls, doll furniture, doll clothes, phone, cleaning utensils

Woodworking—Workbench, tools, soft wood, glue, fasteners, paint, wheels, decorations

Art—Easel, brushes, paints, sponges, chalk, finger paint, collage materials, crayons, clay, markers, drying rack, display areas

Dress-up—Dress-up clothes for male/female and various careers, hats, props like a briefcase or medical kit, puppets, clothes from other lands and cultures

Sand/Water Table—Scoops, sieves, measuring cups and spoons, things that float, things that sink, vehicles, water wheel, things to fill, things that pour, funnel, baster

Cooking—Nutrition posters, measuring cups and spoons, egg beater, bowls, cookbook, spoons, sifter, dull knives, baking pans, blender, hot pads

Music—Rhythm instruments, phonograph, cassette player, records, cassettes, listening center earphones, instruments of other lands, small musical instruments to try

Outdoors—Climbing apparatus, wheeled toys, traffic signs, balls, jump rope, parachute, balance beam

Below are suggestions for learning centers in your early childhood classroom.

Planning Your Day

In planning your daily schedule it is important to remember how children learn best. They are most successful when they are active, when they can integrate several areas of the curriculum into their existing knowledge, and when they have ample time to freely explore. Regardless of whether you work with four-year olds or eight-year olds, your schedule should reflect these ideas.

In order to allow children to be active you will want to schedule time with the learning centers or other activity-based learning. You will want to organize your day into rather long chunks of time so that several areas of the curriculum can be integrated and fragmentation is kept to a minimum. And, you will want to schedule in times of free choice, or at least teacher-structured limited choice, so that children can help in deciding the direction of their learning.

A good day for children should also include a wide variety of learning opportunities. This means there will be active times and quiet times, individual work, group work and whole-class lessons, child-directed and teacher-structured activities, and indoor and outdoor times. Each day should include time for listening, speaking, reading, writing, and thinking. Physical, social/emotional, and cognitive needs should be considered every day. In addition to all of this, most early childhood teachers have specific curricular knowledge they are required to impart, and these skills must be incorporated throughout the day.

The task can be daunting, but by keeping the preceding principles in mind a schedule can include time for everything. Page 28 shows a sample schedule for a half-day program and another schedule for a full-day program. The activities would change according to the grade level, but the basic schedules could apply to any age.

Each day should include time for listening, speaking, reading, writing, and thinking.

Sample Schedules

Half Day

8:15–8:30	Arrival, attendance, organizational activities
8:30–9:15	Free choice from centers structured by the teacher
9:15–9:45	Large group time: story, lesson on theme, introduction of centers, sharing, etc.
9:45–10:15	Snack: preparation and cleanup
10:15–11:15	Small group activities: various centers where lessons are structured around the theme
11:15–11:45	Free choice —either inside or outside
11:45–12:00	Wrap-up and dismissal

Full Day

8:15–8:30	Arrival, attendance, organizational activities
8:30–9:00	Sustained silent reading or writing
9:00–9:45	Literature study— read book, discuss theme, tie to other curriculum, make assignments
9:45–10:00	Recess
10:00–11:30	Language arts integrated block: instruction in spelling, phonics, English, writing mechanics; group reading, individualized reading, journal writing, comprehension discussions
11:30–12:15	Special classes: art, music, P.E.
12:15–1:15	Lunch, recess, read aloud
1:15–1:45	Mathematics: specific skills lessons, tied to other curriculum
1:45–2:15	Content area studies: science, social studies tied to literature study
2:15–3:00	Centers—students rotating among teacher-prepared learning centers supporting curriculum
3:00–3:30	Cleanup, reflection upon day, dismissal

Discipline and Classroom Management

The best discipline is self-discipline, and our classroom management techniques and discipline plans for young children should be focused upon this. However, we know from Kohlberg's (1976) work that young children generally follow rules because they are afraid of punishment rather than following the rules because of internalized ethical values. We also know from Piaget (1952) that young children are egocentric and not able to see another's point of view. The task, then, becomes how to assist children from the egocentric, externally controlled stage of development at which they are to a value-centered, internally controlled level at which they need to function as they grow. To do this we must give children every opportunity to practice the skills of self-discipline. Some ideas for helping children toward self-discipline follow:

The best discipline is self-discipline, and our classroom management techniques and discipline plans for young children should be focused upon this.

◆ Pay attention to classroom climate. The general climate of your classroom should be one of mutual respect and caring among children and adults. No amount of classroom management skills will lead children to self-discipline in a climate of disrespect or coldness.

◆ Model, model, and model. If you want children to speak respectfully, do this yourself. If you want them to learn to take turns, let them see you waiting your turn. Children will learn to abide by rules more readily if they have a model to imitate.

◆ Plan for success. Plan your lessons and activities so that the developmental needs of children are considered. To plan a lengthy, teacher-directed, whole-class activity invites discipline problems for young children. To fail to establish procedures for center use will result in chaos. Children should not be expected to compensate for an adult's lack of sensible planning.

◆ Catch students being successful. Point it out when children are following rules, being caring, or acting responsibly. Schramberg (1988) found that other children not only learn from these comments, but the child who is complimented incorporates this label into his self-concept and behaves accordingly. Unfortunately, children also incorporate negative labels and live up to those expectations, so it is important to focus on positive comments.

◆ Let children govern themselves. No, you are not going to abdicate all classroom responsibility; however, children should be encouraged to help in the development of classroom rules. They should also discuss consequences and rule changes that become necessary as time goes by.

◆ Teach children acceptable alternatives. You will be doing a great deal of indirect teaching by modeling and rewarding responsible behavior. However, sometimes you will want to do some direct instruction on what behaviors are considered appropriate. The teacher who says "Use words—not fists" is teaching a child an acceptable alternative to hitting. Hildebrand (1990) lists distraction, substitution, and redirection as other types of direct instruction which help children to understand social expectations.

The environment in which young children learn is vital to their optimal development.

Concluding Remarks

The environment in which young children learn is vital to their optimal development. This environment should be nurturing, stimulating, and challenging. It should honor the developmental levels and needs of the children and be safe, child centered, convenient, inviting, and active. It can be curriculum based through the use of a variety of learning centers. The daily schedule for young children should also be developmentally based and include a wide variety of learning formats, time for free choice, and integrated curricular times. Classroom management should keep in mind the goal of self-discipline for children and be implemented in a climate of respect and caring.

Becoming Literate

Literacy Takes Many Forms

Imagine a scene in a family room in which three children of different ages are quietly engaged in activities of their own choosing. The oldest, Collin, who is eight, is draped over the couch reading a copy of *Charlie and the Chocolate Factory* by Roald Dahl (1964). One leg dangles haphazardly over the back of the couch. He laughs out loud every so often in response to what he is reading.

The six-year old, Whitney, is busy writing a letter to her best friend who has recently moved away. It is a long and sorrowful letter about all the fun her friend is missing. It starts out like this, "dr Lre. I mis u u are stl mi bsfrn." When she reads the letter to her mother, this part will sound like, "Dear Laurie, I miss you. You are still my best friend."

The youngest child, Morgan, a four-year old, has just gotten a new box of crayons, and she has evidently decided to try every single color in the box. Her sheet of drawing paper has a rainbow, consisting of all 24 colors. Under the rainbow and all along the sides of the paper she has carefully printed M's in all sizes and colors.

Imagine a scene in a family room in which three children of different ages are quietly engaged in activities of their own choosing.

31

Each one of these children falls within the range of early childhood ages addressed in this book; yet, each one is at a very different developmental level and is enjoying a very different activity. The first question we might ask when observing these children is which one is engaging in a literacy activity? The answer, of course, is that they all are. This view, however, represents a radical departure from the way in which literacy instruction was undertaken in the past. For decades, instruction in reading and writing was the business of the first grade teacher. Children were judged to be "ready" for reading instruction when they were about six years old, and the emphasis before that age was on acquiring readiness.

Recently, however, learning to read and write has been recognized more as a journey than a destination. Instead of focusing on a particular point at which readiness is established, the concept of literacy as an evolving and developmental process has gained favor. The term emerging literacy now is used to refer to the process of becoming a literate person. Emerging literacy has been defined as "... the natural, gradual development of a young child's listening, speaking, reading, and writing abilities." (Ollila and Mayfield, 1992, p.1).

> Recently, however, learning to read and write has been recognized more as a journey rather than a destination.

Using this definition, it is easy to see how all of the activities in which Collin, Whitney, and Morgan are engaged can be classified as literacy activities. Morgan has distinguished between letters and pictures and can write the first letter of her name. Whitney has established excellent letter/sound relationships, particularly with consonants, and she has a rudimentary understanding of some punctuation and capitalization rules. Collin has developed a self-direction in selecting his reading material and is evidently comprehending the story well enough to appreciate its humor. None of these activities is more valuable than the others. They are each appropriate literacy steps for the developmental level of the child.

Using the concept, then, of emergent literacy, let's explore what literacy instruction should be in the early childhood classroom. Returning to the Ollila and Mayfield definition above, we see that there are actually four areas of literacy which develop rather than only the traditionally taught areas of reading and writing. In categorizing the types of language we use, we know that sometimes we receive information through listening or reading, and sometimes we express ourselves through speaking or writing. The four ways of communicating can be graphically organized in the simple chart below.

	Oral	Written
Receptive Language	listening	reading
Expressive Language	speaking	writing

All four areas are interrelated and reinforce each other. The base of all of the skills may be the one which actually gets the least attention in classrooms, and this is the skill of listening. We actually spend nearly 50 percent of our days in listening, but very little instruction takes place to improve this skill for children (Kostelnik, Soderman, Whiren, 1993, p. 145).

The oral language skills of listening and speaking provide the foundation for the written skills. Loban (1976) found that children with a weak oral language base also were weaker in written language skills. The Commission on Reading in its report, *Becoming a Nation of Readers*, reinforced the interrelatedness of the four uses of language and advocated the view that instruction in any type of language will strengthen the other types as well (Anderson, Hiebert, Scott, & Wilkinson, 1985). This is good news for early childhood teachers who are sometimes criticized for not teaching reading when actually their oral language activities are fostering reading skills indirectly and appropriately.

The oral language skills of listening and speaking provide the foundation for the written skills.

The concept of emerging literacy makes the question of when to begin reading instruction a moot point. Indeed, reading instruction is a seamless activity rather than a beginning point, and it depends upon the developmental level of the child as to what literacy activity will be the most appropriate. Clay (1975) found that children already know a great deal about literacy before they ever begin formal instruction. Durkin (1966), in a landmark study of early readers, found that these children were just as interested in writing as reading and brought a wealth of literacy knowledge with them when they entered school.

The question, then, shifts from when to teach reading to how to teach reading. As you would expect, there are differing opinions about this. There are three prevailing views today on how to teach young children to read. Let's examine all three.

The bottom-up method is based upon behaviorist theory. This theory states that anything can be broken into very small, discrete parts, these parts can be taught separately, and then they can be reassembled into the complex skills. Using this method, reading is divided into small subskills, such as vowel sounds or the -ing ending. Skills lessons, usually involving worksheets and drills, are developed to teach the desired skill. And, finally, the child is tested on how well the skill has been mastered (Chall, 1983).

The top-down method is focused on comprehension of an entire reading selection. Discrete subskills are de-emphasized in favor of creating meaning and interacting with interesting text. Whole language is often a term used in relation to a top-down approach.

Goodman (1986) states that whole language as a philosophy rejects the teaching of isolated skills and the irrelevant nature of much of the material we ask children to read. Top-down proponents would favor creating a literacy-rich environment and using authentic children's literature to allow a child's natural literacy development to take place. The importance of comprehension over oral reading perfection is also stressed.

The third method is an eclectic approach which takes everything that is best about the other two approaches and uses this in an individualized way to create appropriate reading instruction for young learners. Proponents of the eclectic approach believe in creating a literacy-rich environment and using relevant literature to teach. They also view comprehension as the goal of reading. They do not, however, reject the teaching of skills. The subskills of reading are taught in context and as needed. The developmental needs of each child are used as the basis for the literacy activities which the teacher plans and orchestrates (Manzo and Manzo, 1995).

The literacy-rich environment also includes a respect for language learning.

Of the three methods, the top-down and eclectic approaches are much more conducive to developmentally appropriate practice. Each of these two methods honors the child's needs and prior knowledge. Each easily allows learning to be relevant, active, and child directed. Unfortunately, many primary classrooms and an alarming number of kindergarten and prekindergarten classrooms still have students seated for long periods of time, working on worksheets dealing with isolated skills. Since this is not considered developmentally appropriate practice, let's look at the elements which would be considered appropriate instruction for children emerging into literacy. These elements include: a literacy-rich environment, integration of curriculum, individualization of instruction, relevant reading materials, and appropriate activities.

Literacy-Rich Environment

A literacy-rich environment tends to be noisy and messy. There are good reasons for this. In remembering that oral language is the base for written language, it is clear that a literacy-rich environment will be one which encourages discussion, interaction, and cooperative tasks. In other words, there will be a lot of talking going on. This does not mean the room is out of control in terms of discipline, but it does mean the teacher not only encourages talking but plans for it.

The room tends to appear messy because it is so full of stimulating materials. These would include books and print materials of all sorts, writing supplies, comfortable work spaces, thematic centers, and an explosion of words throughout the room. The results of the literacy work of the children are displayed in every available space.

The literacy-rich environment also includes a respect for language learning. Reading, writing, speaking, and listening activities are part of the daily routine and are used in a variety of ways. Students are actively engaged in increasing their language skills and using this new knowledge to learn in other curricular areas.

Integration of Curriculum

The curriculum in a literacy-rich classroom is integrated rather than divided into specific subject areas. All of the language arts are taught together instead of as separate subjects, such as spelling, English, or phonics. Writing and reading are taught in tandem with the developmental levels of writing being respected. Sulzby (1993) observes that writing ability emerges in a predictable way from scribbling to increasing letter/sound connections to conventional writing. Allowing children to write, whatever their level, will help foster their development.

Besides teaching reading, writing, speaking, and listening in an integrated way, the early childhood teacher also integrates other curriculum, usually through the use of themes or units. Oral and written language, science, social studies, math, and fine arts can all be taught in an integrated way if organized around a theme or piece of literature. This allows children to make connections in the content they are learning. See the ideas on pages 56 and 57 for an example of an integrated literature unit.

The curriculum in a literacy-rich classroom is integrated rather than divided into specific subject areas.

Individualization of Instruction

The teacher in the developmentally appropriate literacy classroom individualizes her instruction to a great degree. However, this is not quite the onerous task it sounds like. The first and easiest way to individualize instruction is to allow student choice. In the scene at the beginning of this chapter no one directed these children to work on their literacy skills. Yet each chose an appropriate task which he or she could accomplish with some success and satisfaction. This also often holds true in the classroom. If the environment is stimulating and accessible, children are frequently very wise about what activities will benefit them best. This does not mean, of course, that the teacher abdicates all responsibility for instructional planning, but it does encourage her to share this responsibility with the children.

Another important feature of successful individualization is that the teacher is well versed in child development and the developmental stages of literacy. With this knowledge (refer to chapter 2), the teacher can plan activities which will be at the appropriate level and have a likelihood of providing success. She will be able to encourage risk taking by her students and feel comfortable with invented spelling and less than perfect products.

Relevant Reading Materials

In order to develop enthusiasm and skill in reading, students must be immersed in print of all sorts. Books of all genres, newspapers, magazines, and functional print around the room are all ways to flood children with words. The printed material should also be of varying degrees of difficulty so that individual children's needs are met. The books should be on a variety of subjects and should be relevant and understandable from a child's point of view. Regardless of the type of books made available to children in the classroom, they should be of high quality. Let's take a short side trip now to discuss how to choose good literature.

Most of the books read by or to early childhood students will be picture books. This does not mean they have no words, although there are a small number of wordless books available, but that they depend in large part on pictures to enhance the story. The most prestigious award given for picture books is the Caldecott medal. In general, books receiving this medal will be of highest quality, though you should still examine these books to determine their appropriateness for your group. A list of Caldecott winners is included on page 73.

There are many fine children's books that do not win the Caldecott, however, and we need a way to critique any children's book we find. Look for the following four characteristics.

1. Writing style and language—Are these of high quality and appropriate for the book? Is the vocabulary understandable yet rich? Are the general elements of plot, characterization, and setting strong?

2. Illustrations—Do the pictures enhance the story? Are they of high quality and suitable?

3. Integrity—Is the story presented in an honest way without talking down to the reader? Are healthy values presented? Are stereotypes avoided?

4. Appropriateness for group—Is the age level suitable? Will the book be understandable to the children you teach? Does it fulfill a need in your curriculum or for a group of students?

Appropriate Activities

The last element of a developmentally appropriate classroom for emerging literacy is the planning of appropriate activities. Since so many activities, like worksheets, copying text from the board, and skill drills are not developmentally appropriate, what activities should we plan to do?

> Most of the books read by or to early childhood students will be picture books.

The International Reading Association (1986), in a joint statement issued with several professional organizations, gives guidelines for what literacy development should look like for young children. Among their recommendations are the following:

- ◆ Present a model for students to emulate.
- ◆ Read to children regularly.
- ◆ Build instruction on prior knowledge.
- ◆ Respect the language of the child.

The first two recommendations can be followed with almost no effort. Reading to children each day from high quality literature is a top priority in an early childhood classroom. Allowing the children to see the teacher reading and writing should be a natural part of each day.

Children should also be writing each day. This builds upon prior knowledge and respects the child's language because it comes directly from the child. Journal writing is a popular activity and can be completely free writing or somewhat directed by the teacher. A list of sample journal topics is included on page 38.

The teaching of phonics skills can be accomplished in a context-imbedded, concrete way which also uses children's prior knowledge. Instead of worksheets to teach sound/letter associations, try teaching phonics through concrete activities which use the child's own language. An example of activities which could be used to teach the letter "f" is on page 39. These activities use a word bank which can be teacher or student initiated.

> **The teaching of phonics skills can be accomplished in a context-imbedded, concrete way which also uses children's prior knowledge.**

Finally, other literacy skills can also be taught in an active way. The activity on page 40 shows how to teach the concept of rhyming without using the traditional worksheets in which the child draws lines between rhyming words. In the Rhyming Words example, the teacher has made the activity concrete and active. It enhances the oral language skills of listening and speaking and builds oral vocabulary in addition to teaching the concept of rhyming.

Concluding Remarks

Emerging literacy is now recognized as a developmental journey that begins long before children become proficient readers and writers. Written language skills will depend heavily on proficiency in oral language. There are three main philosophies on how to take children from oral to written language. These three methods are the bottom-up, behaviorist theory which starts with discrete subskills; the top-down, whole-language emphasis which begins with comprehension of entire texts; and the eclectic approach which integrates skills teaching with the context of literature comprehension. The developmentally appropriate emergent literacy classroom will contain a literacy-rich environment, an integrated curriculum, relevant reading materials, and appropriate literacy activities.

Sample Journal Topics

Children should be given free choice of what to write in their journals. However, for many, simply coming up with a topic is quite a task, so a list of journal topics can come in quite handy.

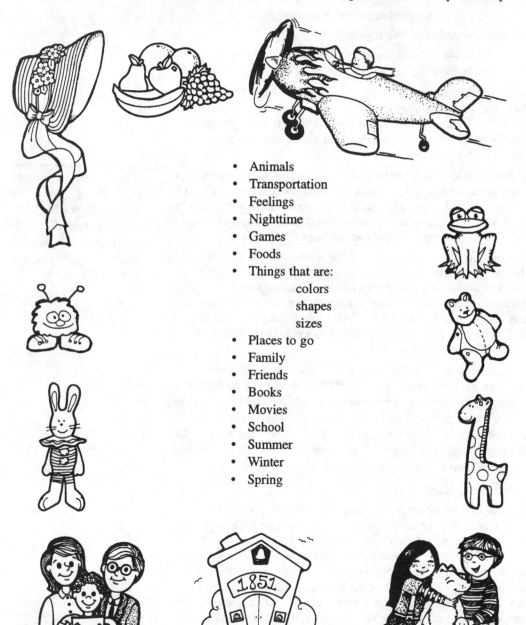

- Animals
- Transportation
- Feelings
- Nighttime
- Games
- Foods
- Things that are:
    - colors
    - shapes
    - sizes
- Places to go
- Family
- Friends
- Books
- Movies
- School
- Summer
- Winter
- Spring

Reprinted from TCM 516 How to Manage Your Kindergarten Classroom, *Teacher Created Materials, 1995*

Using the Letter "Ff"

"F" Word Bank

feel	fib	fiddle	fight	figure
find	float	follow	frighten	fuss
fashion	feast	flood	fancy	false

Activities

1. Talk about animal "feet." Determine which animals have hooves, cloven hooves, paws, webbed feet, claws, toes, no feet, two feet, or four feet.

2. Collect "feathers" for the children to feel. Keep them in boxes or plastic bags. Have the children look at and touch the feathers. Use pictures to show from which type of bird each feather came. This can be done as a center. Children can match the pictures of the birds to the feathers.

3. Make a "fantastic fan" for warm days. Use a small paper plate and a craft stick. Decorate the plate. Glue it to the stick.

4. Discuss "families." Each child has a unique family. Talk about family members. If possible, talk about the students' families to make the discussion more personal.

5. Set up a "fish pond" in the classroom. Put small prizes (pencils, erasers, toys, etc.) into a box or basket. Make a fishing pole with a hook. The hook is made by opening a paper clip and trying it to the end of the string. If the prizes do not have natural places on them for hooking, tie string around them so they can be easily "caught." When a child has accomplished something in the class, reward him/her by letting him/her "go fish" in the pond.

Suggested Reading List

Dauer, Rosemond. *Bullfrog and Gertrude Go Camping*. Greenwillow Books, 1990.

Duke, Kate. *Seven Froggies Went to School*. E.P. Dutton, 1985.

Kalan, Robert. *Jump, Frog, Jump!* Scholastic Inc., 1981.

Langstaff, John. *Frog Went A-Courtin'*. HBJ, 1955.

Lobel, Arnold. *Frog and Toad Together*. Harper & Row, 1971, 1972.

Reprinted from TCM 202 Whole Language Units for the Alphabet, *Teacher Created Materials, 1993*

Rhyming Words

Preparation Time:

One hour

Language Arts and Socialization Concept:

In this activity three-, four-, and five-year-olds experience increased skill in the following areas of language arts: word recognition, rhyming, and word/object connection.

Materials:

rhyming flash cards

What to Do:

In this activity children are exposed to rhyming words while playing a picture rhyming game. This game may be more appropriate for children who are four or five or even six. However, younger children love to take part, and the word recognition and connection between pictures and words is valuable for them. The goal is exposure to many different kinds of learning concepts.

Have children sit in a circle. Pass out the cards. Ask someone to stand up and tell what is on his or her picture. Next, look for a rhyming. There should be 40 different cards and 20 different rhymes. Have children that have matching cards find each other and say the words that they see in the pictures; they will be exposed to rhyming words. You may wish to read a poem that rhymes and talk about how people sometimes use rhyming words to make poems.

Self-Directed Teaching Focus:

Make double-card sets where a rhyming pair is together. Place these where children can play with them at self-directed times, and children will have exposure to the concept of rhyming through pictures.

Directed Teaching Focus:

This game lends itself to circle time and can be used as a directed exercise.

What to Say:

Today we are going to play a game where we look at pictures. It is called a rhyming game. Let's all sit in our circle and look at our pictures. Now, who has the picture of a cat? Great. Tim has it. Stand up, Tim. Who has a picture of a hat? Perfect. Mark has the picture of a hat. Those words rhyme. They end the same. Now let's try some more. Pretty soon, we will all be good rhymers!

Doing More:

Older children can have fun thinking of as many words as possible to rhyme with their picture words (e.g., cat, bat, sat, mat).

Evaluation and Processing Through Storytelling:

Let children write poems and dictate them to you.

Reprinted from TCM 484 Everyday Activities for Preschool, *Teacher Created Materials, 1995*

The Curriculum for Early Learners

Content Area Curriculum

In the last chapter we looked specifically at literacy learning for young children. The bridging of oral and written language and the teaching of reading and writing were given particular attention because these are important, all-encompassing tasks in the early grades. Reading and writing will not be taught in a vacuum, however. Other curricular areas will provide the content for literacy instruction, and the ability to read and write will provide the means to understanding other subjects. In this way, all of the curriculum for early learners is connected and integrated. In this chapter we will discuss these other curricular areas.

Preschool programs often organize their curricula around domains. These broad areas of development would include physical, social/emotional, language, cognitive, and aesthetic learnings. Primary grades are more likely to have curricula arranged around subject areas, such as reading, mathematics, science, social studies, and art. Kindergartens are often given the task of transitioning preschoolers from an integrated day to the more departmentalized approach of the primary grades. In this chapter we will look at cur-

> **Preschool programs often organize their curricula around domains.**

41

riculum as organized by subject but include ways to integrate the subjects to present a unified day which enhances all of the developmental domains.

Before turning our attention to specific subject areas, though, let's review a few principles, based upon the developmental abilities of young children, which will guide all of our curricular planning. The NAEYC provides a great deal of direction about curriculum in its policy statements on appropriate practices for preschool and primary programs (Peck, McCaig and Sapp, 1988; Bredekamp, 1988). A summary of the NAEYC recommendations lists appropriate practices as activities which are concrete and encourage exploration by the child, curriculum which is integrated through the use of themes or projects, teachers who spend the majority of their planning time on preparation of the learning environment, and strategies which encourage cooperation and interaction among children. In each area of the curriculum, then, we might begin by asking, "How can I teach this content in an active, concrete, integrated way which encourages interaction and self-direction by the children?" Ask this question repeatedly as we discuss each curricular area and continue to ask it as you plan your own classroom.

Mathematics

Mathematics instruction undertaken from a developmental point of view emphasizes process over product. Understanding mathematical concepts becomes more important than getting the right answer. There is less emphasis on drill and more emphasis on discovery learning. Content is taught through hands-on, concrete lessons rather than more abstract paper and pencil tasks. Mathematics instruction is a natural part of the day and integrated into other areas of the curriculum.

The National Council of Teachers of Mathematics (1991) has issued standards for the teaching of mathematical concepts. The standards for grades kindergarten through four include skills in problem solving, reason, estimation, numerical operations, geometry, measurement, and fractions, among others. These skills make up the content which is emphasized in the primary grades, and mathematical work in preschool provides the foundations for this later learning. In preschool mathematics instruction emphasizes numbers and number concepts, shapes and forms, patterns and relationships, estimation, classification, and measurement.

In order to teach this content, regardless of level, the developmental classroom will need a multitude of hands-on, concrete manipulatives with which the children can test the mathematical observations they are making. A sample list of materials includes: things to count (buttons, paper clips, bingo chips, etc.) unit blocks, geoboards, tangrams or parquetry blocks, materials for patterning (beads, macaroni, colored paper, etc.), measurement tools (scales, cups, tape measure, etc.), unifix cubes, and rhythm instruments. You will want to look at various areas of the room and consider how to naturally include mathematical concepts everywhere. For instance, the sand and water table can easily reinforce measurement skills through the simple addition of measurement tools to the props available at the table. Most mathematical lessons can be changed fairly easily from our traditional approaches to methods more appropriate for young children.

A sample lesson which incorporates many of the appropriate practices mentioned above is included on page 44. In this activity the skills of patterning and counting are reinforced through a concrete activity. The chart on page 54 also gives an example of a traditional mathematics lesson that has been changed to a more developmentally-appropriate method.

Pattern Jewelry

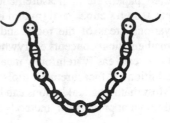

Preparation Time:

Several hours

Math Concept:

This activity introduces three-, four-, and five-year-olds to the concept of patterns through making bead pattern jewelry.

Materials:

an 18" (46 cm) string (thick) or one shoelace per child, large beads of assorted colors (Check out craft stores for a variety)

What to Do:

In this activity children will become aware of patterns by making their own bead jewelry. To prepare for this activity, you will need to decide on the kinds of beads you will use and prepare them. Make sure you have a variety of bead shapes and colors available so children can be creative with their choices.

Model this activity for children by showing them how to string beads and talking with them about all the different color combinations and patterns they can make. After the necklaces are made, compare them and discuss with children how they differ.

Self-Directed Teaching Focus:

Make your bead pattern activity part of your regular craft center. Children may want to make play jewelry on a regular basis. Everytime they string beads a new way, they are creating patterns and becoming aware of the concept of patterns.

Directed Teaching Focus:

Make pattern necklaces for Mother's Day or another gift time. Let each child wrap his/her own gift, with assistance, and take home to give to a family member.

What to Say:

Today we are going to make our own jewelry. Look at these pretty necklaces I've made. Can anyone tell me the two colors I've used on this necklace? Yes, red and yellow. See how first I strung one red bead and then I added a yellow bead? I made a pattern by alternating the beads—red, yellow, red, yellow. Let's all make necklaces, and then we can look at all the colorful patterns we have made.

Doing More:

Make children aware of patterns in everyday activities. Use blocks to make patterns, or use other pieces of toys or games. Take children outside and spend a few minutes looking at cloud patterns or patterns on leaves.

Evaluation and Processing Through Storytelling:

Have children enclose cards with their jewelry gifts. Let them dictate messages for their cards.

Reprinted from TCM 484 Everyday Activities for Preschool, *Teacher Created Materials, 1995*

Science

Many teachers feel frustrated and inadequate when it comes to teaching science. They may not like the subject or may feel they do not have enough knowledge of science to teach it well. Young children, however, do not share these worries. Children are naturally curious about their own bodies and about the world that surrounds them, and that is what science is.

Children are natural scientists. Without direct instruction they have already begun to use the scientific method in learning about their world. They notice something, such as water in a puddle which splashes up whenever they jump into it. They repeat the action many times and in many settings. And they begin to form theories about how the world works. The job of the teacher, then, is to use children's natural curiosity and skill at discovery to provide them with learning opportunities.

The teaching of science in the early childhood years should focus on two areas. The first area is that of process. Children should be helped to develop critical thinking skills and a curiosity about their world. Discovery learning and use of the scientific method should be emphasized. The second area to focus on in early childhood science lessons is specific content. Children need to learn and understand correct scientific concepts in order to make sense of their environment. Both process and content are important in science teaching.

The specific content of early childhood science is generally organized into three areas, biological, earth, and physical sciences.

The specific content of early childhood science is generally organized into three areas, biological, earth, and physical sciences. According to the *California State Science Framework* (California State Department of Education, 1990), each of these areas would reasonably contain many subject areas. Biological science includes plants, animals, human body, and food. Earth science encompasses space, rocks, oceans, and weather. And physical science deals with matter, machines, energy, sound, light, heat, and magnetism.

As with all other early childhood teaching, science lessons should be active, play-based, and integrated into other areas of the curriculum. The content of each area can be taught at any level if done in an active way which honors the developmental levels of the children. A sample of a discovery-based lesson which includes the process skill of observation, which integrates learnings from biological and earth science as well as math skills, and which actively involves children is on page 46. An idea for changing a science activity from traditional teaching to a DAP lesson is on page 54. Science is easily taught in themes, and this is the recommended way of teaching science by the American Association for the Advancement of Science. Pages 56 and 57 show how science content can be integrated throughout the curriculum.

Nature Sort

Preparation Time:

One hour or less

Science and Curiosity Concept:

This activity introduces three-, four-, and five-year-olds to the idea of observation, a foundation of science.

(Additionally, this activity crosses over to math concepts of sorting, matching, addition, subtraction, and counting.)

Materials:

a small paper bag for each child (lunch bags work fine) large pieces of construction paper in a variety of colors

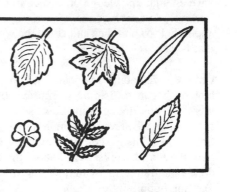

What to Do:

In this activity children collect nature samples and then work together to sort them. To prepare for this activity, all you need is your preschool yard or an available park and a paper bag for each child.

Begin this activity by explaining to children that they will all be collecting interesting items from nature. You may wish to let them know that they may collect only things that are lying on the ground. (This will prevent industrious children from uprooting plants!)

After children have collected a variety of samples, ask each child to pour his or her nature sample onto a large piece of construction paper that will serve as a sorting mat. (To do this activity again and again and save paper, laminate your sorting mats.) Be sure to look over each child's collection for things that should be returned outside, like bugs, worms, or anything your feel uncomfortable sorting.

Next, ask children to separate their leaves into a pile. Then ask children to put their leaves on a separate piece of paper. This will be the "leaf mat." You can have separate mats for rocks, pine cones, twigs, acorns, or whatever else the children find. Another way to sort the items is by color and shape. For example, have children first sort all the green leaves and then all the green leaves that are little. Use words like same, different, big, little, a lot, a few, etc. This will give children a basic science/math vocabulary and begin to set a base for later skills.

You may wish to complete the activity by making mounted displays. Simply glue or paste the samples to the construction paper for a bulletin board or take-home display. Heavy samples may need a little tape.

Self-Directed Teaching Focus:

After the initial direction of the activity, children have a self-directed experience collecting their samples. Be sure to be available to assist them in decision making regarding their samples, etc. Also, if the sorting mats are laminated, this activity can be done again and again and can be placed in your preschool for self-directed play.

Reprinted from TCM 484 Everyday Activities for Preschool, *Teacher Created Materials, 1995*

Social Studies

Social studies includes the study of self and others and the study of culture and environment. Children learn about how they fit into the world. They begin to appreciate all the many beautiful ways in which we are different from one another and also see the ways in which we are alike. They also begin to understand how societies are organized and the expectations of good citizenship within their own society.

The traditional way in which to teach social studies is through a cultural transmissive approach. This approach focuses on commonly held cultural teachings and values. Content includes specific historical facts along with socialization techniques designed to transmit appropriate behavior to children. Another way of teaching social studies focuses on the process of inquiry rather than specific facts and behaviors and requires children to think, reflect, and make active choices. A combination of these two approaches is used in many early childhood classrooms.

Content for social studies includes the subject areas of history, geography, economics, sociology, and government. This content is, of course, translated into lessons appropriate for young children. The traditional way of teaching this content is through a series of concentric circles which extend out from the child in ever-widening spheres of influence. The preschool curriculum, for instance, focuses on the child and family, which the primary grade curriculum widens to include neighborhood and community. However social studies content is organized, though, it should be inclusive and enhance children's respect and appreciation for themselves and others.

Content for social studies includes the subject areas of history, geography, economics, sociology, and government.

The social studies curriculum, and indeed the entire early childhood environment, must emphasize the absence of stereotyping and bias. Children can be harmed through a variety of stereotypes. These include ethnicity, culture, gender, age, family structure, or disability. Early childhood educators should not only encourage the study of diversity but must also actively discourage stereotypical practices in their classrooms.

The practice of asking only boys to help carry objects and only girls to straighten up the housekeeping center is an obviously gender-biased practice. Unfortunately, this practice continues, along with more subtle reinforcements of stereotypes. Teachers of young children must be vigilant in removing these practices from their classrooms and in substituting non-stereotypical books, materials, and activities. An example of a lesson which allows preschoolers to celebrate family differences is on page 49.

Finally, social studies lessons must be integrated throughout the day just other areas of the curriculum are. This is easily accomplished, however, since the topics of social studies blend easily with topics from other subject areas. A lesson in economics, for instance, also becomes a mathematics lesson. A study of ourselves and the things that make us human will also include biological information taught in science. Remember to make all lessons active and child centered. An example of a developmentally appropriate lesson is on page 54.

Family Scrapbook

Preparation Time:

One hour

Self-Esteem and Socialization Concept:

In this activity three-, four-, and five-year-olds gain self-esteem skills through an understanding and awareness of family roles and the differences and similarities in families.

Materials:

one large scrapbook with paper pages upon which pictures can be pasted or glued; old magazines, advertisements, and newspapers with pictures of people

What to Do:

In this activity, children have an opportunity to cut out pictures of families or select precut ones and make a scrapbook of families. To prepare this activity, you will need a large scrapbook with paper pages that can be used with paste. Next, gather a variety of pictures of different possible family groups. Remember to gather a variety of possibilities and stress non-traditional as well as traditional family units. The idea here is to make sure that children have exposure to many different kinds of family groups besides their own. A list of possible combinations that you will want to make available to children to see as families are:

- ❖ family units that include mother, father, children
- ❖ family units that include grandparents living with family
- ❖ single-father family unit
- ❖ single-mother family unit
- ❖ a variety of multi-ethnic combinations: Angelo, Hispanic, Black, Asian, etc.
- ❖ handicapped members in a family unit

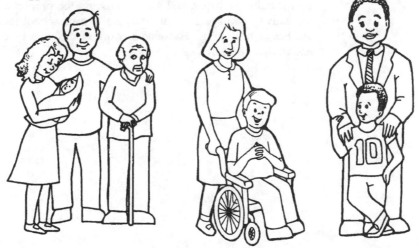

Reprnted from TCM 484 Everyday Activities for Preschool, *Teacher Created Materials, 1995*

Fine Arts

The fine arts traditionally encompass art, music, drama, and dance. Each of these areas needs to be woven throughout the day and made an integral part of the early childhood curriculum. Indeed, it is almost impossible not to include these areas in early childhood classrooms because young children are continually dancing, singing, pretending, and creating.

Taylor (1995) lists seven values that the arts have for children. These include independence, aesthetic appreciation, satisfaction and enjoyment, emotional release, good work habits, muscle development, and exploration. All of the fine arts serve to supply these values to young children. In addition, children often learn other curricular content more easily if it is presented through one of the fine arts. For each of the fine arts it is important that exploration and active involvement are stressed. Some ideas for each area follow.

> **For each of the fine arts it is important that exploration and active involvement are stressed.**

Music

Include songs, finger plays, and rhymes. Make your own music with rhythm instruments or found objects. Listen to different types of music for instruction or enjoyment. Write and compose your own songs. Clap to the rhythm of various songs. Explore musical traditions of various cultures and eras.

Art

Provide a variety of art supplies, such as paints, crayons, pencils, felt-tip pens, brushes, and chalk. Use found items to make a collage; the materials collected for the activity on page 46 could be used for this. Provide opportunities to create from various materials, such as clay, cardboard, paper, and wood. Discuss the properties of color; the activity on page 51 is an example of a preschool lesson which teaches color mixing. Examine artwork of different types and eras and imitate some of these.

Rainbow Watercolors

Preparation Time:

One hour

Science and Curiosity Concept:

This activity introduces three-, four-, and five-year-olds to a variety of curiosity and scientific concepts including: cause and effect, investigation, experimentation, and forming conclusions.

Materials:

twenty plastic cups (clear, not colored), a box of food coloring in assorted colors (red, yellow, blue, green), plastic spoons, butcher paper, tape, paper towels

What to Do:

In this activity children have the opportunity to observe and experiment with different colors. (Please note that this is a messy experiment.) To begin this activity, create a temporary color station. You should have a low, easy-to-reach table, chairs, and a throw-away covering like butcher paper taped to the table top. Next, have a variety of clear plastic cups, plastic spoons, and paper towels. Model the way that colors combine to form other colors. (As a quick review, we have listed easy color combinations for you here:

Typical assortments of food coloring contain blue, red, yellow, and green food coloring. To create additional colors:

> blue + red = purple
>
> red + yellow = orange
>
> yellow + blue = green
>
> yellow + green = lime green

You can also make lighter versions of each of the colors by mixing a lot of water with a small amount of food coloring. For example, you can make pink by adding water to a small amount of red food coloring.

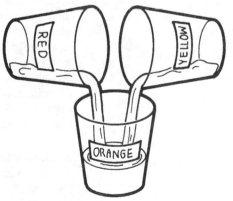

Give children an opportunity to mix colors and see what different combinations they can come up with. Use words that help them to build a science vocabulary - "look," "watch," "let's see what happens," "observe," "changes," "stays the same," etc.

Reprinted from TCM 484 Everyday Activities for Preschool, *Teacher Created Materials, 1995*

Drama

Encourage sociodramatic play through centers in the classroom which invite imaginative activities. Include props and costumes in your classroom for a variety of pretend activities. Write and present your own simple skits. Explore emotions, feelings, and self-concept development through the use of pretend situations. Study examples of drama, such as a video of a children's story, to learn about the elements of the story.

Dance

Listen to different types of music and dance freely to the way the music makes you feel. Explore different types of dance, such as folk dancing or square dancing. Use dance to explore different ways of locomotion and to enhance large muscle development. Explore cultural influences of dance. Create your own dances.

As with all other curriculum, the fine arts should be integrated throughout the day as shown on pages 56 and 57 and they should be taught in a developmentally appropriate way.

Physical Education/Health

Physical activity is an unavoidable part of any early childhood teacher's day. Young children are naturally very active and interested in improving their physical skills, so the job of integrating movement activities into the curriculum is not a difficult one.

Any physical education program will include several purposes. One purpose will be to allow children to gain increasing control over their bodies. Muscular control develops from the trunk of the body outward, from large muscle groups to small ones. This means that young children will be increasingly able to run and jump but less able to control a pencil. Developmentally appropriate physical education lessons will allow children to practice and improve upon their skills. Activities involving balance, locomotion, and hand-eye and foot-eye coordination should be stressed. Children should also be given opportunities to work with a variety of manipulatives. These include balls of different sizes and shapes, bean bags, hoops, and parachutes.

In addition to increasing physical skills, the early childhood program should emphasize physical fitness and wellness. *The California Physical Education Framework* (California State Department of Education, 1986) includes the areas of muscular strength, endurance, and power in physical fitness. It also lists cardiovascular fitness and flexibility as important. Any physical activities for young children should emphasize non-competitive, skill, or fitness-building activities over competitive team sports.

Activities involving balance, locomotion, and hand-eye and foot-eye coordination should be stressed.

Another important component of wellness is health and nutrition. Children in the early years should gain a rudimentary knowledge of a wholesome diet. An easy way of accomplishing this is through cooking and snacks in the classroom. Discussions of healthful foods occur naturally during snack time. Cooking activities which are planned as part of a mathematics or literature lesson can easily double as nutrition lessons.

Other health topics, such as hygiene, dental health, traffic safety, mental health, and first aid should also be integrated into the early childhood day.

Lessons Adapted for Developmentally Appropriate Practice

Traditional Lesson	DAP Lesson
Language Arts	Language Arts
For a lesson on the initial sound of /b/, the child circles all the pictures on a worksheet which begin with this sound.	Instead of the worksheet, the child gathers things from home that begin with this sound and brings them to school in a bag.
Mathematics	Mathematics
For a lesson on counting, the child fills in the blanks on a worksheet like this: 1, 2,___ , 4, ___ 6,7, ___.	Instead of filling in the blanks, the child glues the appropriate number of seeds onto a card which has the numeral at the top.
Science	Science
For a lesson on magnetism, the child reads from a science book and memorizes why some items are magnetic.	Instead of reading and memorizing, the children work in groups with a variety of items and a magnet and generate a list of magnetic items. From this list they make hypotheses about why some things are magnetic and others are not.
Social Studies	Social Studies
For a lesson on communties, the child reads about community helpers in the social studies book and answers the comprehension questions at the end of the selection.	Instead of reading and answering questions, the child designs interview questions for a worker in the community, interviews this person, and writes up the interview to be included in the class community helper book.
Fine Arts	Fine Arts
For a lesson on masks, the teacher cuts out all of the pieces of the mask, constructs a model of the mask, and talks the children through the process so that all of the masks are identical and of display quality.	Instead of a teacher-directed art lesson, the students and teacher talk about the concept of a mask. The children then use found collage items to construct masks which are individual and obviously child constructed.
Physical Education	Physical Education
To build muscle strength and cardiovascular fitness, the children do calisthenics where they not only gain arm strength and cardiovascular fitness but also learn the concepts of over/under and in/out.	Instead of calisthenics and laps, the children engage in parachute play

Curriculum Integration

In all of the curricula delivered in the early childhood years, it is important that the content is woven together into a unified whole rather than being fragmented into subject areas. An excellent way to do this is through the use of themes. A theme can serve as the unifying center for all of the activities in the various curricular areas that take place throughout the day. Themes can be developed around content areas, such as farm animals or dinosaurs or neighborhoods. Or they can be arranged around a piece of children's literature. In either case the teacher starts with the theme and designs learning activities which fit the theme and accomplish the learning objectives of the teacher.

An easy way to begin theme planning is through the use of a curriculum web or cluster. Workman and Anziano (1993) list several ways to envision webs in curricular planning and point out that working with webs helps children incorporate cognitive, affective, and social learning. In designing a web or cluster, simply put your theme in the middle of a sheet of paper. Then let your mind freely explore anything that theme suggests to you. Write down everything you think of. Do not censor any idea or try to arrange the ideas in any logical way. Just get everything on paper. As you do your cluster, follow a three-strike rule to avoid stopping too soon. When your mind thinks it is done, continue on until your mind has stopped three times. The ideas you come up with later in the process are often the most interesting and profound because you encouraged your mind to go beyond the obvious.

An easy way to begin theme planning is through the use of a curriculum web or cluster.

After you have developed a rich cluster around your theme, examine the ideas you have for application to your curriculum. Start with the goals and objectives you have for your children and choose those theme ideas which will meet your goals. Try to choose activities in every area of the curriculum and in various domains of development, physical, social, and cognitive. A cluster and curriculum map built around the book *Ira Sleeps Over* by Bernard Waber (1972) is shown on pages 56 and 57.

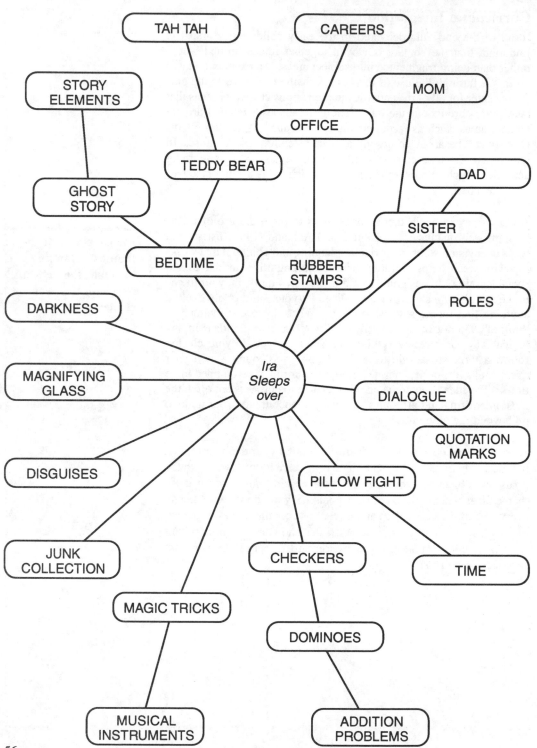

TAH TAH

CAREERS

STORY ELEMENTS

MOM

OFFICE

DAD

TEDDY BEAR

GHOST STORY

SISTER

BEDTIME

RUBBER STAMPS

ROLES

DARKNESS

Ira Sleeps over

DIALOGUE

MAGNIFYING GLASS

QUOTATION MARKS

DISGUISES

PILLOW FIGHT

JUNK COLLECTION

CHECKERS

TIME

MAGIC TRICKS

DOMINOES

MUSICAL INSTRUMENTS

ADDITION PROBLEMS

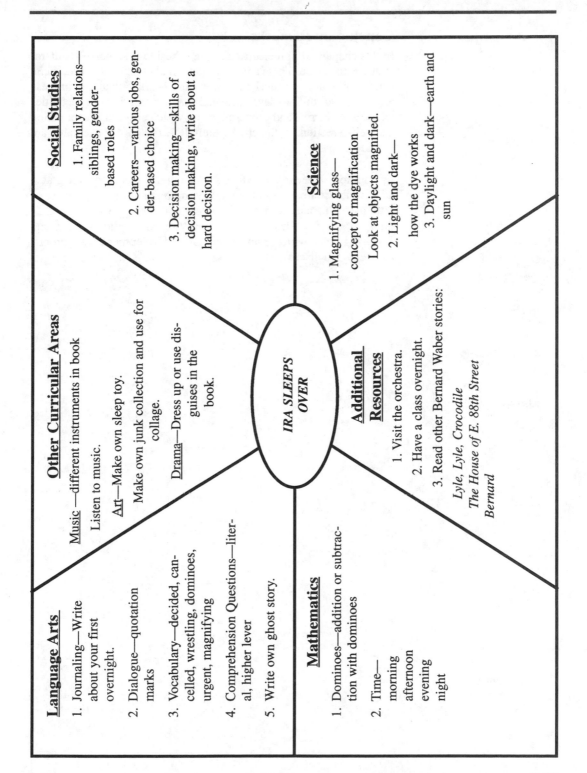

Social Studies

1. Family relations—
   siblings, gender-
   based roles

2. Careers—various jobs, gen-
   der-based choice

3. Decision making—skills of
   decision making, write about a
   hard decision.

Science

1. Magnifying glass—
   concept of magnification
   Look at objects magnified.

2. Light and dark—
   how the dye works

3. Daylight and dark—earth and
   sun

Other Curricular Areas

Music —different instruments in book
Listen to music.

Art—Make own sleep toy.
Make own junk collection and use for
collage.

Drama—Dress up or use disguises in the
book.

*IRA SLEEPS
OVER*

**Additional
Resources**

1. Visit the orchestra.

2. Have a class overnight.

3. Read other Bernard Waber stories:

*Lyle, Lyle, Crocodile
The House of E. 88th Street
Bernard*

Language Arts

1. Journaling—Write
   about your first
   overnight.

2. Dialogue—quotation
   marks

3. Vocabulary—decided, can-
   celled, wrestling, dominoes,
   urgent, magnifying

4. Comprehension Questions—liter-
   al, higher lever

5. Write own ghost story.

Mathematics

1. Dominoes—addition or subtraction with dominoes

2. Time—
   morning
   afternoon
   evening
   night

Concluding Remarks

In this chapter all of the curricular areas besides language arts/literacy were discussed. These areas included mathematics, science, social studies, fine arts, physical education, and health. Planning in these areas should follow developmental theory and include activities which are concrete and cooperative and which encourage exploration and self-direction by the child. Sample activities for each area are included.

In addition, the early childhood curriculum should be integrated across subject areas. A common way to do this is through the use of a theme. Curricula can also be integrated around a piece of children's literature. Ideas for integrating the early childhood day and for changing activities from traditional to developmentally appropriate were also discussed.

Assessment for Young Children

Assessment vs. Evaluation

The terms assessment and evaluation are often used interchangeably by teachers, but there seems to be a subtle difference in emphasis between the two terms. Evaluation often has a judgmental quality to it and leads to the establishment and reporting of grades. Assessment, however, seems to be more concerned with determining a child's skills and needs and planning instruction around this information.

Assessment is defined by the NAEYC in its 1991 policy statement on assessment for children ages three through eight as . . .

> ...the process of observing, recording, and otherwise documenting the work children do and how they do it, as a basis for a variety of educational decisions that affect the child (p. 32).

Using this definition, there is certainly a place for assessment in any program for young children as long as this assessment is done in a developmentally appropriate way. The question then becomes, what constitutes developmentally appropriate assessment? The answer to

Evaluation often has a judgmental quality to it and leads to the establishment and reporting of grades.

that question is that authentic assessment in which children act upon actual materials to demonstrate their knowledge will be most appropriate.

The shift toward authentic assessment in elementary schools recently is due to several reasons, according to Seely (1994). She lists the trend to align learning and assessment, the increase in student diversity, and a feeling of teacher empowerment as reasons for an increase in authentic assessment. Preschools have generally employed more authentic assessment and placed less emphasis on evaluation, and so the elementary grade shift is bringing congruency to all the early childhood levels.

Shepard (1994) extrapolates four guiding principles from the NAEYC policy statement on assessment. They are the following:

◆ No testing of young children should occur unless it can be shown to lead to beneficial results.

◆ Methods of assessment...must be appropriate to the development and experiences of young children.

◆ Features of assessment...must be tailored to the specific purpose of an assessment.

◆ ...The tasks and skills children are asked to perform should reflect and model progress toward important learning goals (p. 212).

Using these guidelines as a beginning, teachers can start to develop appropriate assessment activities for their children. There are many authentic ways to assess a child's understanding of concepts. Let's look at a few of them.

Observation

Observation is probably the most used and least utilized method of authentic assessment. By that I mean that teachers observe children all the time in a variety of settings. However, much of this observation fails to be utilized to its fullest extent. Merely watching children will not automatically yield the information the teacher needs. The observation needs to be focused and recorded to be truly valuable. And it should generate questions and answers for the teacher about what the child knows and needs to know. Traill (1995) advocates a simple stop, look, and listen approach to observation. She recommends that teachers periodically stop and watch children reflectively, look at the behaviors they see and articulate them as precisely as possible, and listen to the children, both orally and in written form, to determine what their needs are.

Observation is probably the most used and least utilized method of authentic assessment.

To be effective, observations need to be focused. A teacher may decide to focus on one child or a group of children for an extended time. Social behaviors or development milestones may be the focus. Or perhaps a specific academic skill will be scrutinized. The point is, the teacher decides what she needs to know about the children and observes with this specific purpose in mind.

The other component necessary to effective observation is the willingness to record what is seen. We all think that we will remember which children on the playground were playing cooperatively or which children still need help with their math facts, but the truth is, we don't. In order for our observations to be useful we need to see them as pieces of the whole picture and look for patterns. Unless observations are written down, memory alone will not be enough to demonstrate these patterns.

There are several ways to record observations. One way is through anecdotal records. An anecdotal record is simply a brief record of observed behavior. The behavior is written down as specifically as possible, and the teacher may wish to add a few words of analysis or reflection. A sample anecdotal entry might be like this:

Kyle chose a book about dogs from the reading corner and spent a full 15 minutes examining the book. He turned the pages correctly and eventually announced that the words under one of the pictures said, "This is a golden retriever." The caption under the picture actually said only "golden retriever."

Comments: Kyle is interested in and knowledgeable about dogs. He knows how to hold a book properly. He understands that written words can stand for meaning. He has good powers of concentration when motivated.

A sample anecdotal record form is shown on page 62. Other methods for recording observations are the running record, the informal reading inventory, and miscue analysis. These techniques allow a teacher to listen to a child's reading, note any miscues that may be made, and analyze these mistakes for patterns. There are many commercially available forms for these assessments. While their administration tends to be somewhat involved, the information they yield is substantial. To learn more about these methods consult *The Whole Language Catalog Supplement on Authentic Assessment* (Goodman, Bird, & Goodman, 1992).

An anecdotal record is simply a brief record of observed behavior.

Individual Anecdotal Records—Example

This is an example of how to keep an individual record of observed behaviors. One of these pages are made for each student and kept in a three-ring binder in alphabetical order for convenient access. When the page is filled up, it can be replaced with a new page and then placed in the student's portfolio.

Individual Anecdotal Record—Example

Name: _____

Date	Comment

Reprinted from TCM 516 How to Manage Your Kindergarten Classroom, *Teacher Created Materials, 1995*

Portfolios

Portfolio building is an increasingly popular way of providing authentic assessment in the early years. A portfolio is simply a collection of a child's work with analysis and reflection upon that work. Portfolios can take several different forms according to Seely (1994), but the two most common are the showcase and the documentation portfolio. The showcase portfolio is a collection of best work. The child and teacher together choose work which demonstrates the child's best efforts. These portfolios are useful for students because they demonstrate potential. They can be made more useful if students reflect upon why they chose each entry and what makes that entry high quality. However, showcase portfolios are of limited value for diagnostics.

The documentation or developmental portfolio is more process oriented. The entries included in these portfolios will not only show best work and finished products but will also show the work that led to the finished product. These might include several revisions of the same paper or writing samples taken at regular intervals throughout the year. These samples must then be analyzed by both student and teacher to determine learning strengths and needs. For instance, a child who wrote in her kindergarten journal "I wnt to mi ants hoos." is giving the teacher many clues about her reading and writing knowledge. She has excellent sound/symbol knowledge for both consonants and vowels. She understands that the sound of "ow" will take some special treatment, though she is unsure about what to do. She understands that I is capitalized and that there is a period at the end of a sentence. The teacher can use this knowledge to plan appropriate lessons for this child.

Entries in portfolios can take many forms. A list of sample entries is on page 64. Whatever you choose to include in the portfolio, though, it should not go unanalyzed. Reflection upon the entries by both student and teacher is the key to better understanding of the child and effective instruction.

Portfolio building is an increasingly popular way of providing authentic assessment in the early years.

What Goes in a Kindergarten Portfolio

As you consider what to put in a child's portfolio, be flexible. As the year progresses, you will think of different areas that could be a part of the portfolio. The children will also have suggestions about what to put in. In the beginning, you will be the deciding factor as to what goes in, but as the children become more familiar with the process, they will want to be more involved. Before you begin, remember one important rule: be sure each item is dated. Always write or stamp the date on each item in the portfolios.

To begin with, you may want to include the following:

Self-portrait

Name sample

Writing sample

Cutting sample

Coloring sample

Math pattern

Dictated story

(This child colors a picture about the story and tells the teacher something to write.)

As the year progresses, repeat the above items for an ongoing assessment. You may also wish to add the following:

Drawings

Taped stories (The child may dictate to show language development.)

Any teacher checklists on the child

Anecdotal records

Homework records/samples

Writing samples

ABC and number learnings

Books read

Paintings

Journals

Parent questionnaires

Special projects the child has done

Cooperative learning records

Audio tapes

Awards, certificates/letters

Reprinted from TCM 516 How to Manage Your Kindergarten Classroom, *Teacher Created Materials, 1995*

Products

One final idea for using authentic assessment is to look at the products which are natural outcomes of concrete, active learning. A young child's captioned painting, for instance, can tell the teacher much about the child's fine muscle coordination, understanding of color and form, and oral language. An older child's mobile built to illustrate a favorite book will allow the teacher to determine whether the child understood the basic story elements of plot, setting, characterization, and conflict.

Products can be a very useful way of determining understanding; however, it will also be helpful to keep in mind Grant Wiggins' (1995) advice to design assessments backward from the task. Wiggins advocates asking whether the assessment activity planned will actually provide evidence of the learning that has taken place. Just because a child produces a concrete product does not mean the products will prove understanding.

Uses of Assessment

There are three main uses for assessment in the early childhood classroom. These three are to plan instruction, to communicate with parents and others, and to identify at-risk students. All of the types of authentic assessment listed can be used for these purposes. For the purpose of identifying children with learning problems which would put them at risk educationally, observation is probably the first tool a teacher will use. The early childhood teacher understands, though, that a very wide range of developmental levels will be present in a classroom, and most children will fall into normal ranges. However, children who are markedly different from their peers will be evident to the teacher and should be referred for specialized testing.

The assessment purpose of communicating to parents and others is traditionally the first use of testing that we think of. However, as important as parental communication is, this is a relatively minor use of assessment. Portfolios, anecdotal records, and other forms of assessment are actually rich sources of information that can be used to communicate a child's progress. It is vitally important, though, that the assessment techniques used in the classroom match the methods used to report progress to parents. If assessment is geared toward observing children and diagnosing their needs for instruction and then the report card calls for letter grades, there will be obvious difficulties and misunderstandings. Letter grades are not recommended by the NAEYC for children in the primary grades. However, letter grades are comprehensible to parents, and it is difficult to move to other ways of reporting. Sperling (1994) reports a promising program in Michigan which links assessment and report-

Portfolios, anecdotal records, and other forms of assessment are actually rich sources of information that can be used to communicate a child's progress.

ing. Her advice is to develop the assessment program and the reporting document at the same time and involve teachers fully in the process.

The final purpose of assessment, planning for instruction, is the most far-reaching and vital reason for assessment in the early grades. Anecdotal records, student work samples, informal reading inventories, and other authentic assessment tools are perfectly conceived as individual diagnostic instruments. Running records of the entire class can be examined to determine skill levels and form flexible groups to teach the necessary skills. A writing sample can provide information that a particular child is ready to move to a new level of literacy. An anecdotal record can demonstrate one child's social skills and suggest how these can be strengthened. The astute teacher can use assessment as a natural part of the spiral of instruction in which assessment leads to instruction which leads to learning which leads to assessment, etc.

Finally, the early childhood teacher should remember the NAEYC caution that if the results of testing will not be used immediately to benefit children, then the testing should not take place. Children and their needs should be at the center of any assessment program, just as they are at the center of all other aspects of the early childhood classroom.

Concluding Remarks

Assessment, like every other part of the early childhood program, should be developmentally appropriate. Authentic assessment is becoming more prevalent and more accepted. Types of authentic assessment discussed included observation and the reporting devices for observation, such as anecdotal records, running records, and informal reading inventories. Portfolios, work samples, and products were also discussed as methods for assessment. The three reasons for assessment, identification of at-risk students, parent communication, and curriculum planning, were explained.

Assessment, like every other part of the early childhood program, should be developmentally appropriate.

Home-School Relationships

Building a Partnership

A kindergarten teacher once complained to a colleague that she had the largest class size in the building. "Why is that?" asked the colleague. "Because I am educating 21 children and about 50 parents when you count stepparents and guardians."

The kindergarten teacher was only half joking. Teachers in the early years will have and should have very close working relationships with the parents of their students. And in many cases, these teachers will be educating parents along with their children. There are many reasons for this, reasons involving the needs of all the participants.

First, parents need to be involved. Many young parents will be sending their first child to school when he/she begins preschool or kindergarten. They need to understand school culture and find ways to be connected to this part of their child's life. They may also need information on parenting during the early school years in order to maximize their child's success.

> Teachers in the early years will have and should have very close working relationships with the parents of their children.

Second, teachers need parents to be involved. Parents know their children better than anyone else and can provide invaluable insights. Parents are their children's first teachers, and teachers need the knowledge parents have and need to capitalize on parents' time with their children to continue the learning environment from school to home. Finally, teachers need as much help as they can get in the classroom, and parents can be a ready supply of adult assistance.

Most importantly, children need their parents to be involved in school. Parental approval or disapproval of school activities will make a great difference in the likelihood of a child's success. The degree to which there is congruence and continuity between school and home can play a major role in how well children adjust to school. According to Powell (1989), mutual home/school support can increase children's academic and physical development. Clearly, children are the big winners when school and home work together. The evidence is so strong in support of parental involvement that the National Association of State School Boards of Education (1988) has made the following recommendations for all programs serving early childhood populations:

> Parental approval or disapproval of school activities will make a great difference in the likelihood of a child's success.

◆ Promote an environment in which parents are valued as primary influences in their children's lives and are essential partners in the education of their children.

◆ Recognize that the self-esteem of parents is integral to the development of the child and should be enhanced by the parents' positive interaction with the school.

◆ Include parents in decision making about their own child and the overall early childhood program.

◆ Assure opportunities and access for parents to observe and volunteer in the classrooms.

◆ Promote exchange of information and ideas between parents and teachers which will benefit the child.

◆ Provide a gradual and supportive transition process from home to school for those young children entering school for the first time (p. 19).

Having firmly established that parents should be an integral part of any early childhood program, let's discuss ways in which to involve parents. These are clustered under the following headings: educating parents, parent communication, the parent conference, and parents in the classroom.

Educating Parents

Especially parents who are sending their first child to school will need some help in understanding the early childhood classroom and developmentally appropriate practice. Parents may ask things like, "All you do here is play; when is he going to learn something?" Or parents may observe, "I see some projects coming home, but when is she going to start to bring home some work?" Parents do not always understand the value of play and the need for concrete activities. The reasons behind these practices must be explained and, sometimes, defended. The earlier teachers begin to explain their programs to parents, the more support they can expect.

Parent education also may include topics like nutrition for growing children, ways to control the television, strategies for dealing with homework, and activities at home to enhance learning. There are many ways to address these topics, such as parent meetings, newsletters, and courses offered through the school. The more parents of young children understand about early childhood development and education, the more they can support and encourage their children.

Parent Communication

One type of parent communication is parent education. However, there are many other reasons and opportunities for communicating with parents. Parents need to understand the specific classroom in which their child functions. What is the schedule like? How is the curriculum arranged? What will be expected of the child? This communication should be ongoing and frequent.

Parents will also need to know about particular events which will be coming up and what roles they could play in these. Field trips, guest speakers, pet days, literary luncheons, and a host of other special events will necessitate specific communications about these happenings. Parent support for these events may be needed in the form of volunteers or help in soliciting donations. But even if no specific help is needed, parents should be informed of these special events.

Finally, teachers need to communicate with parents about the progress of their individual child. In most cases, this should take the form of positive communication. Teachers should begin early and often to let parents know the good things their children are doing. This can be done quickly with a note, a happygram, or a short telephone call. This positive communication, established early, will make the occasional call of concern more effective. Communication about an individual child is often done orally through a parent conference. Some early childhood programs use some sort of reporting form to give written feedback to parents. As long as these forms are developmentally based, they can be useful. The NAEYC does not

> **Communication about an individual child is often done orally through a parent conference.**

recommend letter grades for reporting progress for any early childhood students, including those in the third grade.

There are many, many ways to open the doors of communication to parents. Here is a partial list:

- Introductory letter from teacher—gets everyone off to a good start
- Parent handbook—informs about program
- Newsletter—informs about ongoing events
- Good news notes—quick notes of congratulations
- Personal notes—inform about child's progress
- Telephone conversations—inform about child's progress
- Work packets—collected activities of the week sent home
- Parent center—a place with resources where parents can meet
- School visits—parent sees the child in school environment
- Home visits—teacher sees the child in home environment
- Back-to-School evenings—parents experience child's school
- Parent meetings—parents work together to support school
- Parent workshops—school provides information on parent education topics
- Parent conferences—parent and teacher meet individually

Be sure your communication regularly invites response so that parent-teacher communication is a two-way street.

Parent Conferences

Parent conferences are such an important part of parent communication that they should be given particular attention.

Parent conferences are such an important part of parent communication that they should be given particular attention. Parent-teacher meetings should be recognized as an opportunity for both parties to learn more about the child and establish ways to work together for the good of the child. Even in the most difficult situations, both parties should have the good of the child as the ultimate goal, and this means everyone is working for the same thing.

Parents bring a wealth of information about their child to any conference. They know their child better than anyone else, and they can inform the teacher of the habits, needs, values, and practices of the child. They can explain the home environment and give teachers many insights into their child's behaviors. Teachers, on the other hand, have the opportunity to observe an individual child as a member of a group. And they have the benefit of education in child development and teaching pedagogy. The teacher can give the parent enormous insights into how the child is developing and learning, not only as an individual but also as part of a learning community.

In order for parent-teacher conferences to have maximum benefits, both parents and teachers need to be fully prepared for the event. This means the teacher has gathered all relevant information beforehand and has organized it into some sort of cohesive, understandable package. The teacher also needs to think clearly about what the objective of the conference should be. Parents should also be fully prepared, and teachers can help with this. Teachers can send home sample questions for parents to consider or invite parents to establish their own objectives for the conference.

> **Schools also desperately need adult help in early childhood classrooms.**

During the meeting, teachers should begin on a positive note, remain as positive throughout as is practical, establish a climate of cooperation, and listen carefully to the information parents are sharing. At the end of the conference, summarize the major decisions made and establish next steps. Be as honest as possible, but also be tactful and caring. Remember you both want what is best for the child, and so you are collaborators, not foes.

Parents in the Classroom

Parents of young children need to be in the classroom periodically to understand this new feature of their children's lives. The parent who has visited the classroom will no longer have to ask the vague, unsatisfying question, "What did you do today?" Instead parents can ask much more directed questions like, "What story did you read in circle time today?" Parents with knowledge of the classroom will thus be better able to support and extend what is happening in class.

Schools also desperately need adult help in early childhood classrooms. Volunteers who are dependable and well trained can lower adult/child ratios and make all sorts of special activities possible. Head Start, the federally funded preschool program begun in 1965, has a mandatory parent involvement component which is highly successful, and recently there have been calls for Head Start to extend its partnership beyond parents to other agencies which could provide support. (Administration for Children and Families, 1993–94). No early childhood program can afford to go it alone when there are parents and other adults willing to provide support and strength to the classroom.

Concluding Remarks

There are many reasons why early childhood teachers should forge relationships with parents. The parents benefit through increased knowledge and understanding. The teachers benefit through increased support and help in the classroom. Finally, children benefit through an increased congruency and consistency between the two major portions of their lives.

There are many ways to encourage home/school cooperation. Some of these ways include parent education, parent communication, parent conferences, and parents in the classroom. However parents are integrated into the early childhood program, it is imperative that this take place. Having a truly fine early childhood program without home/school cooperation is nearly impossible.

Caldecott Medal Winners

1938	*Animals of the Bible.* Lathrop		1969	*The Fool of the World and the Flying Ship.* Shulevitz
1939	*Mei Li.* Handforth		1970	*Sylvester and the Magic Pebble.* Steig
1940	*Abraham Lincoln.* d'Aulaires		1971	*A Story—A Story.* Haley
1941	*They Were Strong and Good.* Lawson		1972	*One Fine Day.* Hogrogian
1942	*Make Way for Ducklings.* McCloskey		1973	*The Funny Little Woman.* Lent
1943	*The Little House.* Burton		1974	*Duffy and the Devil.* Zemach
1944	*Many Moons.* Slobodkin		1975	*Arrow to the Sun.* McDermott
1945	*Prayer for a Child.* Jones		1976	*Why Mosquitoes Buzz in People's Ears.* Dillons
1946	*The Rooster Crows.* Petershams		1977	*Ashanti to Zulu: African Traditions.* Dillons
1947	*The Little Island.* Weisgard			
1948	*White Snow, Bright Snow.* Duvoisin		1978	*Noah's Ark.* Spier
1949	*The Big Snow.* Haders		1979	*The Girl Who Loved Wild Horses.* Goble
1950	*Song of the Swallows.* Politi		1980	*Ox-Cart Man.* Cooney
1951	*The Egg Tree.* Milhous		1981	*Fables.* Lobel
1952	*Finders Keepers.* Mordvinoff		1982	*Jumanji.* Van Allsburg
1953	*The Biggest Bear.* Ward		1983	*Shadow.* Brown
1954	*Madeline's Rescue.* Bemelmans		1984	*Glorious Flight.* Provensen
1955	*Cinderella.* Brown		1985	*St. George and the Dragon.* Hodges
1956	*Frog Went A-Courtin'.* Rojankovsky		1986	*The Polar Express.* Van Allsburg
1957	*A Tree Is Nice.* Simont		1987	*Hey, Al.* Egielski
1958	*Time of Wonder.* McCloskey		1988	*Owl Moon.* Yolen
1959	*Chanticleer and the Fox.* Cooney		1989	*Song and Dance Man.* Ackerman
1960	*Nine Days to Christmas.* Ets		1990	*Lon Po Po.* Young
1961	*Baboushka and the Three Kings.* Sidjakov		1991	*Black and White.* Macaulay
			1992	*Tuesday.* Wiesner
1962	*Once a Mouse.* Brown		1993	*Mariette on the High Wire.* McNully
1963	*The Snowy Day.* Keats		1994	*Grandfather's Journey.* Fay
1964	*Where the Wild Things Are.* Sendak		1995	*Smoky Night.* Bunting
1965	*May I Bring a Friend?* Montresor			
1966	*Always Room for One More.* Hogrogian			
1967	*Sam, Bangs and Moonshine.* Ness			
1968	*Drummer Hoff.* Emberley			

References

Administration for Children and Families, Department of Health and Human Services. (1993–94). Shalala calls for refocusing, re-energizing the Head Start program. Children Today, 22(4), 4–8.

Anderson, R. C., Hiebert, E. H., Scott, J. A. & Wilkinson, I. A. G. (1985). Becoming a nation of readers: The report of the Commission on Reading. Washington, DC: The National Institute of Education.

Bloom, B. (1964). Stability and change in human characteristics. New York: Wiley and Sons.

Bredekamp, S. (Ed.). (1988). Developmentally appropriate practice in early childhood programs serving children from birth through age 8. Washington, DC: National Association for the Education of Young Children.

California State Department of Education. (1992). Mathematics framework K–12. Sacramento, CA: Author.

California State Department of Education. (1990). Science framework K–12. Sacramento, CA: Author.

California State Department of Education. (1988). History-social science framework. Sacramento, CA: Author.

California State Department of Education. (1986). Physical education framework. Sacramento, CA: Author.

Chall, J. (1983). Learning to read (updated edition). New York: McGraw Hill.

Clay, M. (1975). What did I write? Auckland, New Zealand: Heinemann Educational Books.

Dahl, R. (1964). Charlie and the chocolate factory. New York: Puffin Books.

Durkin, D. (1966). Children who read early. New York: Teachers College Press.

Elkind, D. (1987). Miseducation: Preschoolers at risk. New York: Alfred A. Knopf.

Erikson, E. (1963). Childhood and Society (2nd ed.). New York: Norton.

Feinburg, S., & Mindless, M. (1994). Eliciting children's full potential. Pacific Grove, CA: Brooks/Cole Publishing.

Goodman, K. (1986). What's whole in whole language? A parent-teacher guide to children's learning. Portsmouth, NH: Heinemann Educational Books.

Goodman, K. S., Bird, L. B., & Goodman, Y. M. (1992). The whole language catalog supplement on authentic assessment. Santa Rosa, CA: American School Publishers.

Hildebrand, V. (1990). Guiding young children (4th ed.). New York: Macmillan.

Hinitz, B. F. (1981). A mini-history of eary childhood education. In J. P. Bauch (Ed.). Early Childhood Education in the Schools (pp. 23–24). Washington, DC: National Education Association.

International Reading Association. (1986). Joint statement on literacy development and pre-first grade. The Reading Teacher, 39, 819–21.

Kail, R. V., & Wicks-Nelson, R. (1993). Developmental psychology. Englewood Cliffs, NJ: Prentice Hall.

Kohlberg, L. (1976). Moral stages and moralization: The cognitive-developmental approach. In T. Lickona (Ed.). Moral development and behavior (pp. 31–53). New York: Holt, Rinehart & Winston.

Kostelnik, M. J., Soderman, A. K., & Whiren, A. P. (1993). Developmentally appropriate programs in early childhood education. New York: MacMillan.

Lawler, S. D., & Bauch, J. P. (1988). The kindergarten in historical perspective. In J. P. Bauch (Ed.). Early Childhood Education in the Schools (pp. 25–28). Washington, DC: National Education Association.

Lemlech, J. K. (1994). Curriculum and instruction methods for the elementary and middle school. New York: MacMillan.

Loban, W. (1976). Language development: Kindergarten through grade twelve. Urbana, IL: National Council of Teachers of English.

Manzo, A. V., & Manzo, U. C. (1995). Teaching children to be literate. New York: Harcourt Brace.

National Association of State School Boards of Education. (1988). Right from the start. Alexandria, VA: Author.

National Council of Teachers of Mathematics. (1991). Professional standards for teaching mathematics. Reston, VA: Author.

National Association for the Education of Young Children. (1991). Guidelines for appropriate curriculum content and assessment in programs serving children ages 3 through 8. Young Children, 46(3), 21–38.

Ollila, L. O., & Mayfield, M. L. (1992). Emerging literacy. Boston: Allyn and Bacon.

Parten, M. B. (1933). Social play among preschool children. Journal of Abnormal and Social Psychology, 28, 136–147.

Peck, J. T., McCaig, G., & Sapp, M. E. (1988). Kindergarten policies: What is best for children? Washington, DC: National Association for the Education of Young Children.

Piaget, J. (1952). The origins of intelligence in children. New York: International Universities Press.

Powell, R. (1989). Families and early childhood programs. Washington, DC: National Association for the Education of Young Children.

Sameroff, A., & McDonough, S. C. (1994). Educational implications of developmental transitions: Revisiting the 5-to-7 year shift. Phi Delta Kappan, 76(3), 188–193.

Schramberg, L. (1988). Child and adolescent development. New York: Macmillan.

Seely, A. E. (1994). Portfolio assessment. Westminster, CA: Teacher Created Materials.

Shepard, L. A. (1994). The challenges of assessing young children appropriately. Phi Delta Kappan, 76(3), 206–212.

Smyser, S. (1990). Prekindergarten: The possible dream. Principal, 69, 17–19.

Sperling, D. H. (1994). Assessment and reporting: A natural pair. Educational Leadership, 52(2), 10–13.

Spodek, B. (1985). Early childhood education's past as prologue: Roots of the contemporary concerns. Young Children, 40(5), 3–7.

Sulzby, E. (1993). I can write! Encouraging emergent writers. Scholastic Pre-K Today, 7, 30–33.

Sutton-Smith, B. (1967). The role of play in cognitive development. Young Children, 22, 361–369.

Taylor, B. J. (1995). A child goes forth: A curriculum guide for preschool children. Englewood Cliffs, NJ: Merrill.

Traill, L. (1995). Highlight my strengths. Crystal Lake, IL: Rigby.

Ulich, R. (1950). History of educational thought. New York: American Book Co.

Vygotsky, L. S. (1962). Thought and language. Cambridge, MA: Harvard University Press.

Waber, B. (1972). Ira sleeps over. Boston: Houghton.

Weikert, D., Rogers, D., Adcock, D., & McClelland, D. (1971). The cognitively oriented curriculum. Washington, DC: National Association for the Education of Young Children.

Wiggins, G. (1995). Grant Wiggins on assessment. Instructor, 105, 16–17.

Woodill, G. (1986). The European roots of early childhood education in North America. International Journal of Early Childhood Education, 18(1), 6–21.

Workman, S., & Anziano, M. C. (1993). Curriculum webs: Weaving connections from children to teachers. Young Children, 48(2), 4–9.

Teacher Created Materials
Resource List

TCM #146	Early Childhood Themes Through the Year
TCM #202	Whole Language Units for the Alphabet (Pre-K–1)
TCM #484	Everyday Activities for Preschool
TCM #516	How to Manage your Kindergarten Classroom
TCM #560	Whole Language Charts for Nursery Rhymes